## Praise for *In Hines' Sight*

Working with Hope Hines for two decades provided me not only with some of the best and most rewarding times of my career, but also an opportunity to attend front and center, an ongoing seminar of "What They Never Teach You in Journalism School." Hope recognized early on that the people element served him better than knowing who was the third-string shortstop of the Padres. That was left up to nerds like me.

MARK HOWARD
FORMER NEWSCHANNEL 5 SPORTS ANCHOR AND CURRENT RADIO
COHOST OF THE WAKE UP ZONE ON 104.5 THE ZONE

*In Hines' Sight* you get the opportunity to walk with "the man behind the microphone" and share the moments, the people, and the lessons God brought his way. It's a great read—get ready to enjoy the journey . . . and don't turn the channel!

LES STECKEL
FORMER HEAD COACH, MINNESOTA VIKINGS,
OFFENSIVE COORDINATOR, TENNESSEE TITANS,
AND CURRENT NATIONAL PRESIDENT, FELLOWSHIP OF CHRISTIAN ATHLETES

Once, as *The Tennessean*'s Vanderbilt beat writer, I was having trouble finding out who would fill a coaching vacancy. Sports Editor John Bibb advised me to hustle, or "Hope's going to scoop your butt." Bibb wasn't worried about any of our other competition. Only Hope Hines. Many times over the years I told him he ought to write a book. Now he has.

LARRY WOODY
RETIRED *TENNESSEAN* SPORTS WRITER, AUTHOR, MARTIN COLLEGE HALL OF
FAME, MEMBER OF THE INTERNATIONAL SPORTS WRITERS HALL OF FAME

I always enjoyed Hope's company. He made me smile. He was unique among sports broadcasters. He made me say things I didn't always want to say, but I knew he would be fair and honest. We have shared many good times together, and I know you will enjoy spending time reading his book and sharing memories from a distinguished career.

**JOHN MAJORS**
FORMER HEAD COACH, PITTSBURGH AND UNIVERSITY OF TENNESSEE

I can think of no better commentator on our shared sports experiences than Hope Hines. Hope always had a smile on his face and he brought dignity to his profession as a six-time Emmy winner. He has had a distinguished broadcasting career, and I am grateful for his work.

**KARL DEAN**
NASHVILLE MAYOR

Through the years since we became best friends at UGA, Hope has been a great influence for good on thousands of 'friends' he doesn't even know.

**CHUCK COOPER**
UGA CLASSMATE, BUSINESS PARTNER, AND FORTY-FOUR-YEAR "BUDDY"

I know you will thoroughly enjoy reading Hope's accounts of forty years as one of the nation's top sportscasters.

**JOE GILLIAM SR.**
FORMER HEAD COACH, TENNESSEE STATE UNIVERSITY

I first met Hope in the '60s when I was writing sports for the *Atlanta Constitution*. Hope was a natural from day one. Solid as he's been professionally, he's proven equally fine as a man. I am pleased he is putting his experiences on paper.

**BILL CLARK**
FORMER SPORTS EDITOR, *THE ORLANDO SENTINEL*

When he was working in television, I considered him to be among the best sports broadcasters in the country. This is a great book that recounts the history of a true American legend in broadcasting. I found it to be a compelling read, and you will too!

**DAVID DAVOUDPOUR**
CHAIRMAN & CEO OF SHONEY'S

I know Hope Hines to be a good person who has always been supportive of charitable and community causes. I'll always consider Hope a good friend.

**JEFF DIAMOND**
FORMER PRESIDENT, TENNESSEE TITANS

5/3rd Bank was a proud sponsor with Hope for several years in his golf tournament. During that time I developed a friendship with Hope which I am proud continues today.

**DAN HOGAN**
FORMER PRESIDENT OF 5/3RD BANK

In the pages of *In Hines' Sight*, you will find stories of success and failure, hope and heartbreak, emotional and relational drama and joy, as well as some personal insights from Hope himself. I know that you will enjoy the read!

**DR. BRYANT MILLSAPS**
PRESIDENT/TREASURER, TENNESSEE BAPTIST CHILDREN'S HOMES

I want to thank Hope, for being an important part of my life professionally and personally. God blessed me with his support and friendship. I know Hope will enjoy retirement with his wife Pat, his kids and friends.

**TOM ERVIN**
FORMER CHANNEL 5 STATION MANAGER

Hope Hines has been our friend, a trusted broadcaster, and a reliable prognosticator. We join with his many fans in applauding his life's work, now on paper.

**BARBARA HAYNES,** RETIRED DAVIDSON COUNTY CIRCUIT COURT JUDGE
**JOE HAYNES,** FORMER TENNESSEE STATE SENATOR

Consistancy, determination, character, and caring. Four words that come to my mind when I think about my friend Hope Hines. When you read about Hope's journey in life, you see how that journey was guided from the start, down fascinating roads, so we can all be entertained and inspired.

**RUDY KALIS**
VETERAN WSMV SPORTS ANCHOR

I have had the privilege of knowing Hope for many years. He has been Nashville's and my favorite sportscaster as well as a huge supporter of Tennessee golf. Hope, have fun playing more golf, and I will look forward to seeing you on the links!

NANCY QUARCELINO
*GOLF* MAGAZINE TOP 100 TEACHER AND
FOUNDER, NANCY QUARCELINO SCHOOL OF GOLF

In my four years with the Tennessee Titans, I got to know and appreciate Hope Hines. Hope was professional and courteous in every aspect of his job. As you read this book, I hope you will enjoy the stories he has to tell; all from forty years of a hall of fame career.

KEVIN MAWAE
SIXTEEN-YEAR NFL VETERAN
(SEATTLE SEAHAWKS, NY JETS, TENNESSEE TITANS);
PRESIDENT, NATIONAL FOOTBALL LEAGUE PLAYERS ASSOCIATION

I doubt Hope ever wanted to be a country singer, but I did have aspirations of a career in sports journalism. Hope got to live my dream, and he lived it well, as you will learn from these pages. I'm proud of his success, honored to call him a friend, but between us, I'm still more than just a little bit jealous!

BILL ANDERSON
GRAND OLE OPRY, COUNTRY MUSIC HALL OF FAME

Hope Hines in his field is like Tom Brady in his field . . . as good as it gets. To be able to read about his life in the sports world—and all the sports figures he's met in that world—will be an experience you will not want to miss.

RAYMOND BERRY
FORMER HEAD COACH, NEW ENGLAND PATRIOTS,
AND MEMBER OF THE NFL HALL OF FAME

One thing will always stand out about Hope. He never waited for the story to break. He was a "digger." To this day, I do not know how he did it, but he always dug up the news item before we scheduled its release. It is rare to speak of icons in the field of local sports reporting. Hope Hines is an icon.

GARY BAKER
FORMER BRISTOL MOTOR SPEEDWAY OWNER, PART OWNER, ATLANTA SPEEDWAY,
AND FORMER NASHVILLE FAIRGROUNDS SPEEDWAY LEASEHOLDER

An amazingly "in-tune" on air personality, Hope Hines from the very beginning became my friend. That's unique in a media world full of cynical people; his transparency is what made him special.

BRAD HOPKINS
FORMER TITANS ALL-PRO LEFT TACKLE

Having been around sports reporters and newscasters most of my life, there is one that sticks out the most! Hope Hines!! Thanks, Hope, for a great twenty years or so that I have known you.

JEFF RUTLEDGE
QUARTERBACK, 1978 ALABAMA NATIONAL CHAMPIONSHIP TEAM,
AND MEMBER OF THREE SUPER BOWL TEAMS

I met Hope Hines in Baltimore more than thirty years ago when I was coaching with the Colts. Throughout all our years of association, Hope was always the consummate sports reporter—knowledgeable, factual, and fair-minded.

EDDIE KHAYAT
FORMER NFL PLAYER AND PHILADELPHIA EAGLES HEAD COACH

The world of sports reporting and commentary has been blessed by the talents of Hope Hines. His personal character and his insights into sports across the board have been rare gifts to all who listen and learn.

WINFIELD DUNN
FORMER GOVERNOR OF TENNESSEE

Hope Hines embodies all that is good in sports broadcasting, and having a chance to witness his tireless effort to bring Nashville a first class show is the highlight of my television experience. Nashville and the state of Tennessee will truly miss Hope Hines.

RICARDO PATTON
UNIVERSITY OF COLORADO BIG 12 BASKETBALL

Hope, you are respected and admired by many people, but no one adores and respects you more than all of us in the music industry. It is indeed with great pleasure that I can call you a friend.

T. G. SHEPPARD
COUNTRY RECORDING ARTIST

A sportscaster with class is how I would describe Hope Hines. A true credit to the community for his many charitable contributions. All young sportscasters could learn from Hope how to be a sportscaster with class.

LARRY SCHMITTOU
FORMER OWNER, NASHVILLE SOUNDS

I was blessed to first meet Hope Hines way back in 1973 when I started on staff with the Fellowship of Christian Athletes here in Nashville. His strong love and bold witness for the Lord have made a real impact on me. I'm proud to be a friend of Hope Hines.

STEVE ROBINSON
REGIONAL DIRECTOR, FELLOWSHIP OF CHRISTIAN ATHLETES
NASHVILLE/MIDDLE TN

The best part about Hope's success is that he has done it all as a class act. I am honored to call Hope my friend and celebrate the success he has had in front of and off the camera. Hope is a Godly man who lives his life as a true inspiration to us all.

GORDON INMAN
TENNESSEE BANKER AND ENTREPRENEUR

Sports fans with foresight should reach to read *In Hines' Sight*, aware that for all these decades, Hope's insight has kept us current on every aspect of professional and amateur sports in Middle Tennessee.

JOHN SEIGENTHALER
FOUNDER, FIRST AMENDMENT CENTER,
RETIRED CHAIRMAN EMERITUS OF THE *TENNESSEAN*

Hope Hines leaves a legacy of excellence in sports broadcasting. He will be remembered for his ethical approach to reporting news, his unique ability to present sports with enthusiasm and clarity, and his comfortable "guy next door" delivery. And now another product of his excellence has arrived . . . *In Hines' Sight*.

BOOTS DONNELLY
FORMER HEAD FOOTBALL COACH AND ATHLETIC DIRECTOR,
MIDDLE TENNESSEE STATE UNIVERSITY,
AND CURRENT EXECUTIVE DIRECTOR OF BACKFIELD IN MOTION

There is a reason Hope Hines was in television for so many years. His wicked smile made viewers tune in to see and hear what Hope knew that they didn't. Over forty years in broadcasting should tell everyone that he was damn good at his job and his viewers loved him.

BRIAN MCKEEGAN
EXECUTIVE PRODUCER OF SPORTS, WTVF-TV

I have remained friends with Hope since our days at the University of Georgia, even after the coach/broadcaster relationship ended. I know you will enjoy his book. It reads like an old friend telling stories.

FRED PANCOAST
FORMER HEAD FOOTBALL COACH,
MEMPHIS STATE AND VANDERBILT UNIVERSITY

There are times in life when a great person emerges in a profession not solely as a result of exceptional skills and amazing talents, but also as a result of their honesty, integrity, and abiding faith. Hope Hines is that person. His accomplishments in the field of sports broadcasting have been exceptional, but what I admire most about Hope is his committed and uncompromising soul. My family and I treasure the wonderful relationship we have had with Hope over the years and wish him God's continued blessings.

HOWARD C. GENTRY JR.
CRIMINAL COURT CLERK, DAVIDSON COUNTY
AND FORMER TENNESSEE STATE ATHLETICS DIRECTOR

# In Hines' Sight

*The Ups, Downs, and Rebounds of
40 Years in Sports Broadcasting*

## Hope Hines

Foreword by Darrell Waltrip

FRANKLIN GREEN
PUBLISHING

In Hines' Sight: The Ups, Downs, and Rebounds of 40 Years in Sports Broadcasting

Copyright © 2012 by Hope Hines

Published by
Franklin Green Publishing
PO Box 51
Lebanon, TN 37088

ISBN 978-1-936487-21-9

Printed in the United States of America
10 9 8 7 6 5 4 3 2

*To Pat*

# Contents

| | | |
|---|---|---:|
| | Foreword | xv |
| | Acknowledgments | xvi |
| | Preface | xvii |
| | | |
| 1 | Is Anybody Listening? | 3 |
| 2 | Glory, Glory to Ole Georgia | 9 |
| 3 | A Music City Welcome | 25 |
| 4 | West Coast Swing | 55 |
| 5 | U-Haul to Nashville, Racquetball, and Saints | 71 |
| 6 | Family Business | 75 |
| 7 | Humpy, Dale, and Dean | 79 |
| 8 | A Baltimore Blast | 85 |
| 9 | Going Home Again | 107 |
| 10 | Music City Duffers and Drivers | 131 |
| 11 | Titans, Preds, and Beyond | 145 |
| | | |
| | Epilogue | 173 |

# Foreword

I met Hope in 1971. He was a rookie just like me.

We did a local TV show called *Pit Stop*, along with his good friend and mine, Joe Carver, the PR director at the Fairgrounds Speedway in Nashville. A lot like his 5+ talk show on cable, it was a show that was fun to do and very relaxed. That's Hope's style, fun and relaxed. Just like me, Hope traveled around the country doing his thing and chasing his dream. That dream was to be the best sportscaster wherever he was working. Hope had some great gigs, from Nashville to San Diego, to New Orleans, to Baltimore. There was something about his style that captivated viewers all over the country, and we were fortunate when he came back to Nashville to finish his career.

Hope's relaxed, laid-back country boy style was perfect for Nashville; after all, he was born in Georgia, and he graduated from the University of Georgia in 1971. His charm and those golden pipes helped make Hope a natural for TV.

This guy is no slow leak either. During his career, Hope won six Emmys and was named Broadcaster of the Year. On top of that, he received an award for twenty-five years of distinguished service in the television industry.

All in all, it's not awards or the success Hope has had that make him special. Hope is real. Hope is honest, Hope is sincere, you can believe him. He never tried to steal the show by being flashy or controversial. He likes to say he was just a regular guy. He is, but he's done extraordinary things with style and grace. Hope Hines is my BFF, and I'm not alone.

Darrell Waltrip
Three-Time Nascar Cup Champion
2012 Nascar Hall of Fame Inductee

# Acknowledgments

To my good friend Ron Cook, who first told me I needed to write a book more than two years ago. I hope you like it.

Along with Ron, God assembled a strong team of encouragers who pushed me to the finish. Stan Moser, an extraordinary mentor. Chuck Tilly, my personal cheerleader in all matters. Stennis Smith, no one ever had a better partner.

Donna, Lyman, and Danny, my children, and whose children, Jordan, Julianne, Ryan, Jack, and Addison are the biggest "big league" players in my life. Jill Hines, my daughter-in-law, who guided me through all the treacherous computer and social network challenges I faced.

To my parents, Lyman and Floreine, you are forever in my heart.

Morris and Tom, my blood brothers, I love you.

Connie Cunningham, my high-school drama teacher, who always told me I was her brightest star.

And I saved the best for last. This book is my story, but it's Pat's too. Just as she has for almost forty years, she guided me with a cool, steady hand, reading every word I wrote, with final approval, of course.

Finally, to all the talented people I ever worked with in television, those in front of and behind the cameras. Thanks for helping prop me up for all those years.

# Preface

Ups, downs, and rebounds. That's been the story of this sports guy's career. It has taken considerable time and distance, but it's been a forty-year "rush" . . . all the way to the finish.

I have been one of the lucky ones who got to do something many people consider a dream job, and it has been. Back in 1971, when it all began for me, I certainly never envisioned my career would last as long as it did or take me to the places I have been.

Along the way I met some incredible people. They were athletes and coaches, ordinary men and women, who accomplished extraordinary things. Their bond, whether teammates or opponents, was the anguish of defeat they all encountered. And the story I told over and over again was how they picked themselves up and continued to chase the wins and records.

A high-five to all those men and women who made my job an absolute joy each and every day.

# In Hines' Sight

*The best day of your life is the one on which you decide your life is your own. No apologies or excuses. No one to lean on, rely on, or blame. The gift is yours—it is an amazing journey—and you alone are responsible for the quality of it. This is the day your life really begins.*

BOB MOAWAD

# 1

# Is Anybody Listening?

GEORGIA • JUNE 1962

THE FIRST TIME I FLIPPED that microphone switch to on, my life made sense. Up until that moment, I was pretty much going nowhere.

There were Georgia pines taller than the radio tower that carried WSFB's radio signal from Quitman, Georgia, across the flat farmland of Brooks County.

I would choose one of the top country songs of 1962—Bill Anderson's "Mama Sang a Song," Marty Robbins's "Devil Woman," or maybe Hank Snow's "I've Been Everywhere." Then I would quickly reach across the turntable and cue up a reel-to-reel tape commercial for Patrick Furniture Company. The trick then was to rush out the back door of the small concrete block building before the song ended and feed the station owner's horses, who had been calling for their breakfast with their noses pressed against the glass in the back door.

I was a twenty-year-old "morning man" on a 250-watt radio station in my hometown, wondering, *Is anybody listening?* and having the time of my life.

Two years earlier, I had graduated from high school, and I attended Columbia Military Academy in Columbia, Tennessee, in the fall of 1960 as a post-graduate student. I was not a model student, and I certainly was not a model cadet. I left CMA one very cold January night in 1961. I just walked out the back gate, bought a bus ticket, and went home to Quitman.

By the time I arrived, my parents Lyman and Floreine had been notified I was AWOL, and the greeting I received was not warm.

### ❖ Mama Was Not Happy

My father was a respected businessman who owned an International Harvester truck and tractor dealership. My mother taught high school. My junior year I took one of her classes, creating a certain amount of agony for both of us.

I enjoyed being a cut-up, and on one particular day I was especially full of myself. She had already corrected me for talking in class. Then she called me down again.

"But, Mama," I pleaded. That's when she ordered me to the principal's office, with a stare Pat Summitt would have been proud of. You see, at the beginning of the year Mama had instructed me never to call her *Mama* in class. So there I was, heading down the hall to the principal's office, but it was a certain image of my father that weighed heavily on my mind.

The principal was a pretty hip guy, and when I got to his office and told him what had happened he burst out laughing, which was certainly a relief for me. He said it was one of the funniest things he had ever heard of.

Still, all I could think about was how my father was going to react. I knew he would be incapable of finding any humor whatsoever in my mother's classroom embarrassment when he got home that night, and I was right.

There were two more at home just like me, my younger brothers, Morris and Tom. Needless to say our poor mother had her hands full.

### ❖ My Circle Grew to Three

After my return home from military school, the next major event in my life took place when I married my high-school sweetheart.

School was simply not on my radar at that point. I spent the next year splitting time working for my father and my father-in-law, a prominent Brooks County farmer. There was not very much about farm life that appealed to me, and working for my father was not terribly exciting either. The excitement in our lives, however, did pick up considerably when our daughter, Donna, was born.

Not only did I play sports in high school, I also acted in school plays, and during my junior year I had decided I wanted to be an actor when I graduated. That didn't happen, of course, but it was because of acting that I applied for that radio job, and to my great surprise, they hired me.

I loved to press the earphones from my headset tight against my ears to better hear myself.

"Up next . . . here on the breakfast club, this one is for all you folks droppin' in at the Royal Café for that first cup of coffee. It's Claude King and 'Wolverton Mountain.'"

I worked Sundays as well, from sign-on until noon. Sunday mornings, Pastor Harland Lester and Sister Beulah May (I never did know her last name) would show up at eight o'clock for their live gospel music and preaching hour.

The small studio had a microphone on a stand in the middle of the floor and a stand-up piano against the wall. My, how Sister Beulah May's fingers would fly across the keyboard. They would sing a verse, then stop and plead for money, then they would pick up where they left off with the singing. Listeners were encouraged to send for their prosperity "prayer-cloth" . . . for a five-dollar donation, of course.

When the singing (very good), preaching (very little), and pleading (very much) were over, Pastor Lester would come in the control room, hand me ten dollars for the half hour, and walk out with a grin, saying, "Ain't God good."

There was another youngster getting his start in radio in Quitman the same time I did. Mike Harvey hosted an afternoon rock-n-roll top-forty show at that time, and he later went on to national radio fame on Saturday nights, coast to coast, as host of *SuperGold*.

### ❖ Hope the Sportscaster

It happened late on a Thursday afternoon in early September. Station owner Bill Hoopes casually asked me if I thought I could do play-by-play for a Brooks County high school football game the following Friday night.

I had played football in high school, so I guess Bill assumed I'd be able to describe what was happening on the field. I was not about to let this opportunity slip away, and besides, at twenty you pretty much think you can do anything. So my quick response was "Yes, sir, I'm pretty sure I can," followed by one of those dumb question mark smiles.

I will not bore you with details of how dreadful that first play-by-play broadcast was, but I am happy to say there would be better days ahead for me in the broadcast booth.

God bless the farmers, I just wasn't meant to be one of them. I'd settled happily into my new role as a radio DJ. Quitman was a small town, and that's okay for those who love small towns, but I knew my opportunities would be limited if I stayed, and now I began to think about a college education.

In 1964, I enrolled at Madison Junior College in Madison, Florida, thirty miles south of Quitman, where I continued working in radio.

### ❖ I'm Gonna Be a "Dawg"

In the summer of 1965, a classmate and friend told me he was driving to Athens, Georgia, for an appointment with the University of Georgia dean of students. He hoped to transfer to Georgia and invited me to ride with him. He suggested I should bring along my transcript as well.

I had never entertained any thought of going to Georgia. Florida State was my school. Tallahassee was only sixty miles from Quitman, and I had been a Seminole fan all my life, attending many football games at Doak Campbell Stadium. But something told me I should make that trip and take my transcript, so I did.

It was a long trip back . . . for my friend. He was turned down. I was accepted. He wound up transferring to another school, and I enrolled at Georgia in the fall of 1965.

## In Hines' Sight

Remarkable things happen when you least expect them, and for me, this was one of those moments of surprise when a revelation of extraordinary significance is revealed. It is often in these moments that we come face to face with who we are or who we think we are. For a long time, I had no idea who I was—or, more importantly, who I could be—until the doors of the University of Georgia swung open for me.

I knew I had not been called to ride a tractor all day in the hay fields for my father-in-law or to work for my father at the dealership. There just was no joy for me in those pursuits.

The talents God had given me were in a totally different "field." Settling for what you have, I'm afraid, is what too many of us do because of . . . fear and circumstances. We tell ourselves we're not good enough. It will be too hard. What will my family and friends think? I don't have enough time. It will cost too much. There are a thousand fears keeping us from trying something. But remember what Alexander Pope said . . . "An excuse is worse and more terrible than a lie; for an excuse is a lie guarded."

Determine as soon as possible what you are good at. When you do, you will never work a day in your life. You'll be having too much fun.

The beginning of self-discovery and passion for me happened at that little radio station in 1962.

And that's how a fifty-year career in broadcasting began for a guy who had been listening for years to such nighttime voices as John R and Hoss Allen on WLAC in Nashville, Dick Biondi on WLS in Chicago, and several voices I can't remember on neighboring stations in Valdosta. I would lie awake at night wondering if I would ever have a radio career outside of Quitman . . . population 4,562.

*There are many things in life that will catch your eye, but only a few will catch your heart . . . pursue those.*

MICHAEL NOLAN

# 2

# Glory, Glory to Ole Georgia

## ATHENS • 1965–1971

SINCE I WAS MARRIED WITH a daughter, I needed to work while going to college, and I was obviously hoping I would find something in radio in Athens.

As luck would have it, a high school classmate of mine and former WSFB announcer was at Georgia, and he was also working at a local station.

With his help, I landed a job at WGAU in the summer of 1965 as a mid-morning DJ and began working for station owner H. Randolph Holder, who as best as I could tell wrote the book on radio. He was a wonderful teacher and mentor in all aspects of the business.

But ask Country Music Hall of Famer Bill Anderson what he thinks about H. Randolph Holder, and you'll get this story. WGAU was a middle-of-the-road music station. No rock, no gospel, and certainly no country. While attending journalism school at Georgia, Bill worked for Randolph as a DJ. Bill, of course, knew the policy, but from time to time he would slip in a country song, and more than once he was told to stop. And then it happened. Bill played a country song one day at the worst possible time, and Randolph was not in a particularly good mood that day.

He fired Bill. Bill and I have laughed many times over the years about his misfortune in Athens radio.

One day in late summer of 1965, Randolph asked me if I had ever done play-by-play.

"Yes, sir, I have," I replied, trying to contain my excitement.

That fall, I took my sportscasting career to the next level as I began doing play-by-play for Athens High School football, basketball, and baseball.

## ❖ Learning from the Pros

My football broadcast hero was the legendary Larry Munson, who had just taken over the football play-by-play duties for Georgia. Larry and I became friends, and our paths would cross many times over the years. I will explain later how he was instrumental in helping me secure a play-by-play job on a fifty-thousand-watt station.

Milo Hamilton and Munson were the broadcast voices of the Atlanta Braves, but unbeknownst to most, the two men hated each other. I was introduced to Milo by my friend Bob Montag, the former home run king for the old minor league Atlanta Crackers. To my delight, Milo invited me to join him and Munson in the broadcast booth at Atlanta Fulton County stadium on several occasions. It was a wonderful learning experience for me, and I took those opportunities to immerse myself in the smallest details of how the two men orchestrated their broadcasts.

## ❖ Road Buddies

It was during that first 1965 season of broadcasting Athens High football that I struck a deal with a young sportswriter with the *Athens Daily News.* He and I attended journalism classes together at Georgia and became friends. I invited him to join me on the broadcasts to keep game stats while doubling as a color commentator. His name was . . . Lewis Grizzard.

Lewis wanted to be a syndicated newspaper columnist, and I wanted to be a TV sports broadcaster. We each achieved our goals. Lewis became a popular and much sought after Southern humorist, with his columns appearing in more than 450 newspapers across the country. He made numerous appearances on national television, and he earned a well-deserved reputation as one of the country's best stand-up comedians. Before his death in 1994, related to lifelong heart issues, Lewis penned twenty-five books. Nobody loved the University of Georgia more, and in my heart, Lewis Grizzard will always be Georgia's "Top Dawg."

I will always cherish my conversations with Lewis as we traveled those North Georgia hills covering Athens High sports. Talk about starting at the bottom of your profession! One day Lewis and I broadcast a high school baseball game from inside a wooden maintenance hut, just beyond the outfield. We sat on stacks of fertilizer sacks as we called the game. Many times we sat in the stands alongside the fans when we called basketball games.

We were two college students working our way through school, both with interesting marriages (we both would be challenged by holy matrimony more than once) and both very ambitious about our careers.

Over the years, we played many rounds of golf together. The winner bought the beer. Even with a five-dollar limit, we both became very skilled at stacking beer cans pyramid style.

Lewis graduated before I did and went to work for the *Atlanta Journal*, leaving me without a color analyst for the radio broadcasts. That's when Dallas Tarkington (brother of former NFL quarterback Fran Tarkington) came to the rescue. Dallas and I became lifelong friends, and his passion for radio inspired him to own multiple AM and FM stations over the next twenty-five years.

Another member of the traveling radio team was station sales manager Tip Almond, who was there to protect his interest: the commercials. He had sold most of them. Tip became my best friend. He not only guarded and guided my college broadcasting years, but he supported and helped me in so many ways, like a big brother.

## In Hines' Sight

Each of us goes through phases in our lives during which friendships help steady our course. I have been blessed with a number of close friends who were pillars of strength and encouragement during difficult times. Unfortunately, it took years before I would fully understand how priceless those relationships were.

The June 2006 issue of *American Sociological Review* featured a study that showed that close friendships were deteriorating. The research revealed that 25 percent of Americans have no close friends. How sad.

The people who have impressed me the most, more than any accomplishment they might have had, are those who have embraced faith, family, and friendship as their greatest fortune.

C. S. Lewis, in *The Four Loves*, writes: "To the Ancients, Friendship seemed the happiest and most fully human of all loves; the crown of life and the school of virtue. The modern world, in comparison, ignores it."

I also love what Ralph Waldo Emerson wrote: "It is one of the blessings of old friends . . . that you can afford to be stupid with them."

## ❖ A Friendship Forged on the Links

Time passed, and I continued going to school and working lots of hours at the radio station each week. My son, Lyman, was born in 1966, and the pressure of work, marriage with two children, and school began causing problems in all three areas.

I was attending classes on a major college campus, and, perhaps unavoidably, I began to be somewhat influenced by the revolutionary "counterculture" of young people who condemned convention and authority and who freely experimented in drugs and sex. The war in Vietnam was also raging.

In 1967, I met a young man while playing at the University of Georgia golf course. He absolutely blew me away—not with his game, although he played very well. It was his looks. He had been burned on over 70 percent of his face and body. His appearance was horrible, but his personality was energetic and sparkling. He told me his story, and right then and there, Paul Jenkins became the most remarkable person I had ever met. I listened, horrified, as he detailed a painful and gruesome description of what had happened to him one summer afternoon several years before.

Paul's father owned a crop-dusting business. His machine of trade was a World War II open-cockpit, single-propeller biplane. The technique was to fly low, with the wheels almost touching the crops (cotton, soybeans, tobacco, etc.), as he sprayed chemicals and pesticides from the back of the plane.

Paul had learned to fly during high school so he could help in the family business during the summer months. He had been home from college that July, and on the day of the tragedy he was making his final pass over a field as the sun was setting. He turned to look behind him, making sure the spray was even. Lost in concentration, he lingered too long. Just as he turned around, pulling back on the stick, the plane nosed up, heading into the sky, but the wheels became entangled in some telephone wires and the plane flipped end over end, crashing into a pine thicket.

The plane's fuel cell exploded on impact, and gasoline sprayed all over Paul's body. He was literally on fire, and he told me that the odor from his burning flesh made him vomit. That and the pain. He said he could hear the cartilage in his nose and ears crackling as flames engulfed his neck and face. He tried to unfasten his seat belt, but the hot metal peeled the skin off his hands. A pine sapling had fallen across the open cockpit, and Paul was pinned. By now the pain was excruciating, and he began to lose consciousness.

Something sparked inside, however, and his instinct for survival took over. He didn't remember exactly how, but somehow he knocked a hole in the side of the cockpit so he could escape. He remembers falling to the ground and rolling in the dirt to extinguish the flames, as most of his clothing had been burned away. By now the agony was almost too great to endure.

He found himself walking through the woods and finally stumbling onto a dirt road. Standing in the middle of the road, his body now swollen because of the burns, and not thinking clearly, he heard the rattle of a pickup truck approaching. As he turned to face the sound, the old man driving the truck almost ran into the ditch at the sight of Paul.

The gentleman helped Paul into his truck, and they drove to the nearest county hospital, where the staff was ill-equipped to handle such injuries. Paul was taken to an Atlanta hospital, where the decision was made to transport him, by private jet, to the world-famous burn center in Houston, Texas.

Paul described the scene as the plane was flying at thirty thousand feet somewhere between Atlanta and Houston. A highly skilled team of doctors and nurses was fighting for his life, when he heard one of the doctors say, to no one in particular, "This man has one chance in a million of surviving this flight."

Paul said that when he heard the suffocating words of that doctor, his spirit cried out. "God, until now you have not been a part of my life, but if you will let me live, I promise to spend the remainder of my days serving you, however and wherever you lead me."

Of course, Paul did live, and for the next several years he was in and out of hospitals for countless surgeries to his face and body. The doctors did the best they could, but his face had been burned severely, and he was hard to look at . . . until you got to know him.

Now comes the good part. The perfection God performed for Paul Jenkins had nothing to do with skin tone. God's miracle for Paul was that he healed him from the inside out, and the result was the greatest positive attitude I have ever witnessed.

"Hope," he said, "I know I'm good-looking. Every time I walk down the street, everybody turns and looks at me."

There's no way you could ever feel sorry for Paul. He had found something special. A relationship with God and his son Jesus Christ. I am happy to say that the bond I formed with Paul, and the lessons he taught me by example, helped begin my own spiritual journey with God.

### ❖ Decision Time

Because of my association with Paul Jenkins, and his influence, I began reading the bible. Which book of the Bible would you say is the book you do not want to read first? Revelation? Bingo. That's where I began. Big mistake.

I worked the mid-morning shift at the radio station, and every Wednesday R. Gene Payne, a Baptist minister, delivered a fifteen-minute devotional at noon. Gene was a big sports fan, and over several months we developed a friendship. Of course, I was a captive audience for his weekly devotional, since I was the one turning the knobs in the control room.

One day following his devotional, I told Gene that I had been reading Revelation and that I was totally confused. I told him I had absolutely no idea what the book was talking about, and I wondered how anyone could figure it out. He smiled and said he just might have a few keys to its understanding. He asked what time I got off work. I said in about an hour, and he said he would meet me outside.

When I walked out of the station after my shift, I had forgotten about our meeting . . . until I saw Gene sitting in his car in the far corner of the parking lot.

I climbed in and closed the door. After some small talk, he began to read some passages from the Bible. It was during those few minutes that I realized I needed to turn my life over to Jesus Christ, and I did.

I will not tell you being a Christian is easy. It is not. I have slipped, stumbled, and fallen many times over the years in my walk with Christ, and by God's grace I continue to be a work in progress.

---

## In Hines' Sight

---

The following is adapted from an essay on friendship by Alvin C. Romer:

People come into our lives for a reason, a season, or a lifetime. When someone is in your life for a reason, it is usually to meet a need you have expressed. They have come to assist you through a difficulty, to provide you with guidance and support, or to aid you physically, emotionally, or spiritually. They may seem like a godsend, and they are. They are there for the reason you need them to be.

Some people come into our lives for a season, because your turn has come to share, grow, or learn. They bring you an experience of peace or make you laugh. They may teach you something you have never done. They usually give you an unbelievable amount of joy. Believe it—it is real. But only for a season.

Lifetime relationships teach you lifetime lessons, things you must build upon in order to have a solid emotional foundation. Your job is to accept the lesson, love the person, and put what you have learned to use in all other relationships and areas of your life. It is said that love is blind, but friendship is clairvoyant.

I am glad and wish to thank you for being a part of my life, whether you were a reason, a season, or a lifetime. Only time will tell.

### ❖ On the Field Training

It was while covering Georgia athletics, specifically football and basketball, that I learned to conduct interviews.

I would go to football practice with my tape recorder (remember this was the '60s), watch practice, listen to the newspaper reporters ask questions (there were never any TV stations covering practice), and wait my turn. There was a definite pecking order, and guess who came last.

One of the writers I especially admired was Bill Clark, who wrote for the *Atlanta Journal-Constitution* and later became the sports editor of the *Orlando Sentinel*. Bill always found time to talk with me. I figured it was because I covered practice everyday and could help him with information, since he only came to Athens once or twice a week. Bill and I formed a friendship that has lasted through the years. He and his wife, Betsy, are retired and living just outside Murfreesboro, Tennessee, where he grew up. Bill is one of the best "senior" tennis players in Tennessee.

Legendary Georgia football coach Vince Dooley was the first head coach I observed up close, and what I learned from watching and listening to him during those early years impacted me for the remainder of my career.

Vince was all business—in fact, it was two years before I knew he could smile (wonder where Derek Dooley gets that trait), and as a young reporter I was intimidated by him. He ran his football program like a corporation, and he was the hands-on CEO. I would occasionally ask a dumb question, but he was always gracious enough to give me an answer, though perhaps with a trace of sarcasm if the question lacked the proper thought process.

As a Vince Dooley observer I witnessed the consistency of his personality. Smooth and even-keeled, with a sharp football mind, Vince had been a history major at Auburn and often sounded more like a professor than a coach. Discipline was the absolute backbone of his program, and any slip would land a player in his "Dawg" house. I greatly admired the man, and beyond all the awards, titles, and championships, Vince Dooley became the model by which I measured integrity.

On Dooley's staff was another legendary coach in the making. Defensive coordinator Erskine "Erk" Russell, who died in 2006, was one of my all-time favorite people. I could devote an entire chapter to Erk, but then he would have asked me, "Why not two chapters?"

How do you not love a guy whose passion for coaching was always on display? That fire and emotion escalated to new heights one day at practice when he slammed his bald head into a player's helmet after a key play. The impact left Russell's forehead dripping with blood.

A master motivator, Erk coined the phrase "Junkyard Dawgs" as inspiration for his undersized defense following Georgia's poor 1974 season. Erk was also a skilled promoter. One day he suggested to Roger Dancz, director of Georgia's Redcoat Marching Band, that when the Bulldogs did something really good on the field they should crank up a few bars of Jim Croce's "Bad, Bad Leroy Brown."

One of my proudest accomplishments during those years at Georgia during football season was syndicating a weekly thirty-minute radio show with Erk Russell to stations across the state, and believe me, there was never a dull show with Erk.

In 1981, Russell was hired as head coach at Georgia Southern, where he was responsible for resurrecting a program that had been dormant for forty years. The Eagles would win three NCAA Division I-AA national championships during his eight-year tenure.

One more Erk Russell story: In 1986, Maryland basketball player Len Bias was drafted by the Boston Celtics as the second overall pick, but he died two days later because of a cocaine overdose. When Russell read about Bias's death, he called a meeting with his Georgia Southern football team. His purpose was to convey the dangers of drug use. How did he choose to convey this message? By throwing a live rattlesnake on the floor, telling his players that messing with drugs was just as deadly as picking up that snake. Anybody doubt he got his message across?

# ❖ Wrong Information

It began as an early career highlight for me, but it quickly turned into an embarrassing low moment. Following the 1966 season, Georgia earned a trip to the Cotton Bowl to face SMU.

WGAU radio in Athens, where I worked, was a CBS affiliate and would carry the Georgia-SMU game on December 31. The station was sending me to cover the game, and I decided to call CBS radio in New York to offer my services as their Georgia play-by-play "spotter" for the broadcast. I talked to their game-day producer, who told me Harry Caray would be doing the play-by-play and they would be happy for me to spot for Mr. Caray. At that time, Harry was the legendary announcer for the St. Louis Cardinals, but later, he would of course become the lovable, iconic broadcaster for the Chicago White Sox and Cubs.

You can imagine how thrilled I was to get to sit beside Caray, who was already considered one of the country's broadcast giants.

I was instructed to get in touch with Harry when I got to Dallas to arrange a pregame meeting. I called his hotel and was told he was accepting calls in the bar, which seemed quite appropriate since he already had a reputation for drinking and partying. When he answered the phone, there was so much background noise I could hardly hear him. We spoke briefly, and he said I should meet him in the broadcast booth two hours before kickoff. I was telling him how excited I was to be working with him when he abruptly hung up. Had to get back to the party, I figured.

Game day arrived, and we met in the booth at the appointed hour. Harry had his spotter boards filled out with players by position, and he told me how he wanted me to communicate with him during the broadcast. A spotter's job, using the board, is to point out the ball carrier and who makes the tackle on any given play.

We settled in as the game got underway, and I was understandably nervous to be working with such a famous guy. Added to my excitement was the fact that the game was being nationally broadcast. Then it happened. Second play of the game. The handoff was to Georgia tailback Kent Lawrence, who broke to the sidelines on the far side of the field and raced for a seventy-four-yard touchdown run. The only problem was . . . I pointed to the incorrect ball carrier on the spotter board! Harry Caray then told the nation he

In Hines' Sight

had just witnessed one of the most exciting touchdown runs he had ever seen and praised the blinding speed of . . . the wrong player. Oops! I wanted to die.

During the commercial break I got a well-deserved, profanity-laced reprimand for my blunder, as only Harry Caray could deliver it.

Years later, while working in TV in Baltimore, I interviewed Caray, who by then was broadcasting White Sox games, and reminded him of that Cotton Bowl game and my horrible mistake. He didn't say a word and just looked at me for the longest moment. Then his face slowly broke into that well-known Harry Caray smile, and he burst out laughing. Seeing his reaction that day was indeed a special "Moment of Hope."

## ❖ Decision Day

A few months before graduation, I called Ed Thilenius, the former football play-by-play announcer for Georgia, who was now the sports director for WAGA-TV, the CBS affiliate in Atlanta. I had been watching him for several years and had met him on several occasions. I asked him if I could visit the station and observe how he prepared for a sportscast. He graciously consented, and several weeks later I arrived at the station early one afternoon and was ushered into his office.

I was greeted by the future head football coach at Alabama and later Kentucky, Bill Curry. Bill was anchoring the weekend sports that summer before he returned for training camp as a Pro Bowl center with the Baltimore Colts. What a thrill it was to meet him. A genuinely nice guy, Bill played college football at Georgia Tech and had worked at the Atlanta TV station for several summers.

I watched Curry and Ed Thilenius go about their duties preparing for the six o'clock news and knew, without a doubt, that somehow, someway, I would become a TV sportscaster. I just didn't have the slightest idea how that was going to happen.

## ❖ Graduation, Now What?

Attending the University of Georgia and working in radio will always be one of the grandest experiences of my life. But graduating in 1971 from the Henry Grady School of Journalism was definitely an epic day for me. It had taken me six years to graduate. I had quit school for almost two years to work full time. All of the important people in my life were there: my wife and children, my parents, and my great friend and mentor Tip Almond, who for the past year had loaned me the use of a car . . . otherwise I would have been walking to class.

### ❖ Help, I Need a Job

It was the end of June, the euphoria of graduation had long passed, and the reality of looking for a job, any job, was . . . job one.

Every week, the journalism department at Georgia posted available jobs in radio-TV, newspapers, magazines, and public relations from around the country. I went by almost every day to check on the prospects. TV sportscaster? I never saw one posting. In order to feel like I was at least doing something, I applied for several public relations jobs, which I thought I might be good at. Weeks went by, and I heard nothing.

It was time to think about plan B. There was only one problem: I didn't have a plan B. Heck, I didn't even have a plan A. Now what?

I talked to my friend Chuck Cooper, who had graduated from graduate school in journalism the year before. He was the assistant to the dean of the university's agriculture department. But he couldn't help.

I went to see Bill Simpson, another friend, who was head of the university's public relations department, but he couldn't help either.

I had contacts with the Atlanta Braves and Falcons, but I struck out there too. By now several students I had gone to journalism school with had gotten entry-level jobs at various places. After many weeks of anxiety, I didn't need a doctor to diagnose what was happening to me. I understood exactly what was going on.

It was called job panic.

Late one afternoon, after stopping by the journalism department and once again finding nothing on the job board, I dragged myself home, prepared to spend the evening having one of the finest pity parties you ever saw. Instead, my wife met me at the door and informed me that Dr. Worth McDougal, head of the radio-TV department at the university, had called and left his number.

My first thought was, Okay, what could Doctor Mac possibly want? "It's too late to call tonight. I guess I'll call him tomorrow," I said.

The next morning, his secretary answered the phone and put me on hold. Just what I needed, more suspense. Then I heard, "Hope, I have something you will be interested in."

Relief. Instant relief.

"I want you to call Chris Clark in Nashville, Tennessee. Chris is a Henry Grady graduate and is the news director at WLAC-TV. He called yesterday saying they had an opening for a sports anchor. He asked if I had any recommendations, and I gave him your name. He's waiting for you to call him."

I couldn't believe what I was hearing! Sports anchor . . . Nashville, Tennessee . . . WLAC-TV. Wow!

"Yes, sir, I certainly will . . . and thank you, Dr. McDougal. Wow!"

I called Chris Clark, and he told me that Dr. McDougal had given me a very good recommendation. Chris knew I had no experience in TV, but he asked if I would send him a videotape of my work in front of the camera at school. I did have some video of me anchoring sports for a television class, but it was horrible, and I had no intention of letting him see that. So I did some quick thinking.

"Uh, Mr. Clark," I said, "it just so happens that I will be in Nashville next week." (This was not true, but I figured I would make it true!) "Would it be possible for me to stop by the station and see you in person?" I closed my eyes tight, fearful of what he would say.

"That will be fine," he replied. We set the day and time for my visit.

### ❖ Channel 5 Interrogation

One week later, I walked up the steps at 474 James Robertson Parkway and entered the station lobby. The next several hours were the most intense I had ever experienced. I was interviewed by Chris Clark, station manager Harold Crump, program director

Bill Jay, sales manager Tom Ervin, and weather personality Bob Lobertini.

They put me on camera and had me read some wire copy. When I was done, Bill Jay, standing just off camera, suddenly threw me a "frisbee" and said, "Sell it. I want you to adlib a thirty-second spot." Talk about pressure.

At one point during my conversation with Bob Lobertini, he let it be known that I was competing for the job against guys (in 1971 there were no women doing sports) who had years of experience anchoring on television. Thanks, Bob, I needed to know that.

Late that afternoon, I had a final meeting with Chris, who said some very nice things about my audition, thanked me for coming, and said he would be in touch.

I walked back to my car thinking, "Sure you will. I'll never hear from you again."

I was wrong. Two weeks later, Bill Jay called and said they would like to bring me back for a second visit, and they would send plane tickets for me and my wife. Things were getting serious, and I was getting really nervous.

My second interview was very much like the first. I talked to the same people, saying pretty much the same things I did during the first interview process, except this time I was introduced to station owner Tom Baker. He had very nice things to say about all of the other nice things everybody else had to say about me. I don't think he ever saw my audition tape. I sat there in his handsomely decorated office as he helped me understand what a privilege it would be for me to work for WLAC.

My final meeting of the day was with Chris, Bill Jay, and Harold Crump. There were a few minutes of small talk, then Chris caught me totally off-guard when he said, "We'd like to offer you the job. When can you start?"

It was one of those "freeze-frame" moments, as my world came to a complete stop. Shocked, I couldn't speak at first. Then I think I muttered something like, "Are you sure?" Then I said, "Today! I can start today." Everybody laughed, we shook hands, and I walked out in a trance, thinking "How did I do that? How did I get this job?"

Would you believe I had no idea what they were going to pay me, and guess what? I didn't care. I don't even remember if money

In Hines' Sight

was mentioned, and I never asked. I wasn't about to sweat the small stuff.

### ❖ The Worst Fifteen Minutes of My Life

When I returned to Athens I called all my family and friends with the incredible news.

The next day . . . I got the call.

"Hello, Mr. Hines, this is Joyce with Western Union Telegraph. May I read you this urgent message from a Mr. Chris Clark, WLAC-TV, Nashville, Tennessee?"

"Yes, ma'am, please do," I said, feeling a little nervous and gripping the phone tighter.

"Due to internal strife, offer of employment as 'sports anchor' must be rescinded . . . further explanation will be forthcoming. Thank you, Mr. Hines," she said, and hung up.

A bomb had just exploded in my hand. I was totally shell-shocked. I couldn't breathe. I couldn't swallow. I couldn't think. It felt like a two-thousand-pound bull had just kicked me in the gut. Tears began rolling down my face. A thousand thoughts crashed through my brain, all bad. What possibly could have happened? What went wrong? This can't be, I thought.

I phoned my wife, who was at work. "They just fired me," was all I could say.

"What are you talking about?" she replied, with tension in her voice.

"I just got a telegram from WLAC. It said they had to retract their offer. I've got to call them. I've got to find out what happened." I hung up.

I sat there for a good fifteen minutes, trying to collect my thoughts and get up the nerve to make the call. Suddenly, the phone rang again.

"Hello, Mr. Hines, this is Joyce with Western Union again. I have a second message for you. 'Gotcha!'" Then nothing but dial tone.

It took a few seconds to register, and then I leaped out of the chair, punched the air with my fist, and shouted, "Chuck Cooper, I will kill you, dead!"

The phone rang again. This time I grabbed it without hesitation, and before I could say hello, I heard, "Gotcha!" Chuck was roaring with laughter on the other end. I couldn't help but laugh as well. He finally explained that he had had his secretary make the Western Union calls, and he wanted to know my reaction.

I told him, in no uncertain terms, to kiss me where the sun don't shine. My good friend Chuck had just pulled off one of the all-time best practical jokes, ever. We have laughed many times about that moment over the years, and I can promise, he continues to watch his back, because he never knows when I will return the Gotcha.

## In Hines' Sight

Thinking back, I consider the years 1965 to 1971 to have been my six years of basic training for the life adventure I was about to embark on. They were hard years, fun years, educational years, and years I spent shaping and sharpening the passion that fired my soul.

I am smiling as I write this, reflecting on those experiences as a wonderful time of discovery and self-realization. It was a time of early experimentation with the gifts and talents God had given me. I wasn't afraid to try anything behind a microphone. Oh, sure, some of the things I did came off stupid and ill-conceived, but even those mistakes gave me a certain thrill and rush. And yes, I made lots of mistakes—usually the result of poor decisions. But it was, in so many ways, the best time of my life. I love what Ray Bradbury, author of more than five hundred literary works, said: "Living at risk is jumping off the cliff and building your wings on the way down."

I would continue to build my wings for the duration of my career. And, so . . . if you're ready . . . here come forty years of career highlights.

"Roll the tape, J.B."

# 3

# A Music City Welcome

## NASHVILLE • 1971–1975

M Y VERY FIRST TIME ON television in Nashville was a memorable one. I kept glancing at myself in the monitor next to the camera as I read the sports. I thought I was looking pret-tee good.
Now, I ask you: who wouldn't stare at the monitor their first time
on TV?

I am indebted to the late Channel 5 weekend weathercaster
Ron Kiser, who graciously instructed me in the art of applying
makeup. Guess what I don't miss after forty years? Pancake and
powder. Brushes and blush. And do you have any idea how much
hairspray I used in all those years? Neither do I, but I've been told
former Dallas Cowboys coach and Fox analyst Jimmy Johnson and
I have a lot in common. And my wife, Pat, said I always looked like
I was wearing a frisbee on my head because of the way I combed
and sprayed it across the front. Thanks, dear.

❖ The "King" and I

In 1971, *Monday Night Football* was a year old. *Gunsmoke* was in its
sixteenth year. Walt Disney World opened in Orlando, and
Richard Petty was the "King" of Nascar.

It was July, and the week of the Nashville 420 Nascar Winston

Cup race at the Fairgrounds Speedway. I had been on the air less than a week, and I was riding with the station's veteran news photographer Milton McClurken to the Speedway to conduct my first interview.

We drove in the back gate and through the tunnel to the Speedway infield. There were no "haulers" in those days. Drivers or crew members usually pulled their race cars behind a pickup truck. We parked the news car in the middle of the infield, and I had my first look at the famed five-eighths-mile oval Speedway. It already had a great reputation as a favorite short track among the drivers.

As Milton was collecting his camera from the trunk just a few yards away next to an infield light pole, I could see a crew member working under the hood of a car. From where I was standing, all I could see was the guy's backside and his legs, which were tucked into ankle-high boots. Then I noticed the car. It was blue. Not just any blue, mind you, but the "43" Plymouth Petty blue. That's when he came out from under the hood, holding a wrench in one hand and a carburetor in the other. He glanced at me and smiled: Richard Petty, bigger than life.

He didn't say anything and quickly disappeared back under the hood. By now, I had a belly full of butterflies. Several other people, probably crew members, were crowded around, peeking under the hood. Their conversation was muffled, but there was no mistaking Petty's voice.

Suddenly, he reappeared and leaned against the car, wiping his hands with a rag. Milton began shooing B-roll, first of Petty, then various shots of the car. Milton was going about his job with precision, while all I could do was watch in awe.

It took Milton about ten minutes to get the shots he wanted, then he motioned for me to join him. Petty was standing there joking with some guys, and we waited for him to acknowledge us. Five minutes later back he went under the hood.

That's when Milton took charge of the situation. He placed the camera on the ground and leaned under the hood. "Mr. Petty, when you get a moment, we'd like to do a quick interview, if you don't mind."

"Be just a minute," he responded.

In Hines' Sight

Remember, this was my first-ever TV interview. Milton handed me the mike and told me where to stand. Right about now I was hoping Milton could also do the interview. My mouth was dry, and my heart was beating like a hummingbird.

"All right, fellows, what can I do for you?" That Petty smile definitely eased the tension, and after introductions I did my first television interview with the King. I'll never forget it. I won't say it was better than my first kiss, but it came pretty close. He responded to my questions, as primitive in substance and unpolished as they were, as if I were a seasoned pro. Your first is always special, and Richard Petty will always hold a special place in my sportscaster heart.

Over the years, two of my all-time favorite people to interview have been Arnold Palmer (more about Arnie later) and Richard Petty. Beyond their skills in their respective sports, it's not hard to understand why they have been so successful as superstars. It's how they treat their fans and interact with the media, on good days as well as bad.

My first Richard Petty encounter was the perfect learning experience for a novice reporter. It taught me if the King could be nice to a TV nobody then every other high-profile sports celeb could just as easily be nice to the nobodies of this world.

### ❖ The Early Edition of "Jaws"

There was another racing legend in the making in the early '70s. And unlike Petty, he was brash, brazen, audacious, cocky, impulsive, and . . . LOUD.

Darrell Waltrip moved from Owensboro, Kentucky, to Franklin, Tennessee, in 1970 with his new bride, Stevie, to begin his storied and often controversial Nascar career.

I met Darrell in 1971 on a Saturday morning at Channel 5 on the set of a show called *Pit Stop*. Darrell was the guest, and I had inherited the host role. I knew very little about stock car racing, but with Darrell I didn't need to know anything, because he knew *everything*. Darrell would ask the question and then answer it himself! We did that show every Saturday with Darrell and Joe Carver, who would later become Darrell's manager.

None of the other drivers would guest on the show. They were intimidated and afraid of being on camera. Not Darrell. Oh, no. He loved it from the start, and the camera loved him. He was smart, quick-witted, and well-spoken, and the best part was that he wasn't afraid to make fun of the other drivers, especially the ones who gave him the most competition week to week. It made for great TV, and more than that, it helped fill the stands at the Speedway on Saturday nights. The more Darrell ran his mouth, the bigger the crowds. Half the fans loved him—the other half despised him. Fairgrounds promoter Bill Donoho might have been the only one having more fun than Darrell. Every time Darrell opened his mouth on TV, Donoho saw dollar signs.

One of the first drivers Darrell made fun of was Coo Coo Marlin, Sterling's father. DW would say something like, "Coo Coo? Coo Coo! What kind of name is that?" and burst out laughing.

One Saturday, Darrell was in rare form and was even more outrageous than usual as we taped *Pit Stop*. When the show ended, I joked that he was fast becoming the Muhammad Ali of racing. Darrell's quick response was, "I'm pretty sure I can't stand toe to toe with Ali, but I sure as heck can go jaw to jaw with him." Little did we know that day what a big role "Jaws," would play in Waltrip's career. And believe me, I'm not done with DW; not by a long shot. The Waltrip saga continues in later chapters.

## ❖ A Snowy-Showy Ride to Daytona

Before February 1973, I had never ridden in a limousine. Then came those five days and fifteen hundred miles in a limo. Boyd Adams, a former driver at the Fairgrounds Speedway in the '60s, owned a limousine company in Nashville. We were both friends with Joe Carver, the PR director at the Speedway. Joe came up with the idea of us traveling to Daytona in a limo with Boyd, for the purpose of getting some pre–Daytona 500 interviews that I would then air in Nashville as part of the lead-up to the 500.

It was a great idea, and I was definitely excited about riding to Florida in style and comfort in a stretch limo. We left Nashville following the ten o'clock news on a cold and wet February night. Boyd was driving, Joe was riding shotgun, and I was in a deep sleep on the long back seat. Suddenly, Joe leaned over and said, "Hope, you need to wake up. It's snowing."

We were just south of Atlanta, passing through Forsyth, Georgia, on Interstate 75. I looked at my watch. It was almost 3:30 a.m. Several inches of snow were already on the road, and the traffic (mostly eighteen-wheelers) was bumper to bumper. Abandoned cars and trucks were left in various angles along the side of the road.

There had been no snow in the forecast that night, and everyone had been caught by surprise. None of us had packed heavy clothes. Remember, we were headed to sunny and warm Florida! By now, the Interstate was clogged and traffic had stopped completely. The three of us got out of the limo and looked around. Other travelers had done the same. Those with multiple passengers began pushing their cars from behind though the snow. We decided that was a good idea. Boyd would drive, and Joe and I would push. I'll never forget the next several hours pushing a limo down Interstate 75 in three or four inches of snow. It didn't take long for my feet to freeze in my thin socks and loafers. The heaviest coat I had was a windbreaker. Joe didn't have anything heavier either. The only bit of good news was that we had filled the gas tank in Atlanta.

The Interstate was filled with passengers in one car getting out to help other cars that were stranded. Many times during those hours, Joe and I would get behind a vehicle and push to get the car back on the road. The looks we got when we stepped out of the limo were, shall we say, amusing.

By 6:00 a.m., we had made it almost to Macon, about twenty miles from Forsyth. The snow had stopped, but the road was almost impassable. Time to stop, rest, and regroup.

We parked on the side of the road and all three of us passed out, exhausted, for the next two hours. Boyd was in the front seat, and Joe and I were in the back. We woke up to the sun streaming through the windows and the sound of crunching snow as vehicles moved slowly down the Interstate.

We fired up the limo and got back into the slow caravan of cars and trucks headed south. It had snowed all through Georgia, and we arrived in Daytona the next afternoon . . . and crashed.

Funny thing about riding around in a stretch limo. When people see you drive up, they get really curious. We had fun with it on more than one occasion. One night we drove to a popular restaurant at Daytona Beach and circled the establishment several times so that everyone got a good look at the limo. Of course they were all burning with curiosity. The restaurant was packed, and people were standing around outside waiting to get in. Just as Boyd pulled up in front, Joe bounced out and quickly opened the back door. I stepped out and angrily began berating Joe for not getting me to the restaurant on time. Joe apologized, acting completely ashamed and embarrassed. I continued my verbal assault, making certain I had everyone's attention. Then I stopped, took a deep breath, looked slowly around at everyone looking at me, and said harshly to Joe, "And as for Petty (Richard) . . . who needs him? Call Allison and tell him to meet me here in thirty minutes. I then stormed through the crowd of stunned onlookers and disappeared inside.

Boyd, Joe, and I laughed about that all the way back to Nashville. Mrs. Cunningham, my high school drama teacher, would have been proud.

### ❖ A Big "John" Greeting

"Hey, baby," came the booming voice as soon as he spotted me in the Channel 5 hallway. "I heard you were in town. Just wanted to come by and introduce myself."

With at least a twelve-inch "stogie" in his left hand and a John Wayne stride, John Merritt greeted me with a warm handshake and a big smile. It was the beginning of a very special relationship.

John Ayers Merritt was, quite simply, unforgettable. His enormous personality was undeniable. He made everyone around him feel significant . . . a rare gift, indeed.

So special were his motivational skills that he recruited the top black kids in the South to play football for Tennessee State University, offering them the dream of one day playing in the National Football League. Their names included Claude Humphrey, Eldridge Dickey, Jim Marsalis, Cleveland Elam, Ed "Too Tall" Jones, Joe Gilliam Jr., and Richard Dent, who was inducted into the NFL Hall of Fame in 2011.

A Merritt trademark was assigning his favorite players a nickname. Eldridge Dickey was one of the best quarterbacks the nation never saw in the late 1960s. Merritt called Dickey "The Lord's

Prayer" because, as Merritt said, "Every time he steps on the field, he delivers." The story goes that in one particular game, Tennessee State trailed 36-3 at halftime. In the second half, Dickey led a furious comeback, and when the game ended, the scoreboard read, "The Lord's Prayer 37, The Opposition 36."

Some of the other nicknames Merritt bestowed included Joe "Turkey" Jones, Lawrence "Bad News" Barnes, Joe "747" Adams, Nate "Suitcase" Simpson, Richard "Dirty" Dent, and, of course, "Jefferson Street" Joe Gilliam.

Merritt, by his own admission, left the coaching to his two top assistants, defensive coordinator Joe Gilliam Sr. (father of "Jefferson Street" Joe Gilliam) and offensive coordinator Alvin "Cat" Coleman. Merritt's primary roles were raising money for the football program, recruiting, and making sure his boys got their lessons and graduated. On the football field, he was the master motivator. He could often be seen sitting in his cigar-smoke-filled, autumn-rust Cadillac beside the dusty practice field observing his team at work. By the way, John never drove himself anywhere. He always had a chauffeur. Shorty was his favorite. Wherever you saw John, you saw Shorty.

During his twenty-year reign as head coach at Tennessee State, Merritt became a member of the 200 Club, made up of coaches who have won two hundred or more games in a career. Merritt was head coach at Jackson State for ten years before coming to TSU. Big John won more games (234-67-11) than Bo Schembechler, Hayden Fry, Jake Gaither, and Vince Dooley.

He often joked he could have won more, but integration killed his recruiting when the big schools began signing the kids he usually got without much effort.

### ❖ The Best Show on Nashville TV

One of the great joys of my forty-year TV broadcast career was hosting the *John Merritt Show* on Sunday mornings. During football season, it was the highest-rated local TV show on the air. Two words, and two words only, describe why more people watched that show than any other . . . *John Merritt*.

The show was always live, which meant there were no "do-overs." Several times throughout any given season, John would be late for the show. I would begin by recapping Saturday's game, telling the audience I was sure John would show up any minute, and "stretching," as we call it in television. Finally, John would enter the studio, and as he was walking to the set he would bellow, "Tell 'em I'm here, baby!"

Then, like a big bear (six feet two inches and about 275 pounds), he would fall into the chair next to me, still talking without his mike on.

When the mike was finally in place, the first thing John would do was reach in his coat pocket, pull out a long Cuban cigar, and light it. Merritt would inhale deeply and then very slowly exhale the smoke, which would form a cloud just above our heads, but not out of the camera's eye. It hung there like a grey halo. At home, the audience was absolutely loving it.

"Hope," he would begin as he adjusted his large frame in the comfortable lounge chair, "tell ya why I'm late, baby. One of my boys' mama is sick in the hospital in Birmingham. I had to round him up and bring him to my office so he could talk to her on the phone. We just got done, and I rushed over here as soon as I could. I apologize for being late."

For the next five minutes, John would talk about what a fine lady the player's mama was and how proud she was that her son was playing for Tennessee State University. "That young man don't have a thing to worry about, 'cept going to class and playing football. Big John's making sure his mama is well taken care of, and I've assured him she's gonna be just fine." By now the hearts of the viewers belonged to John, and with the remaining time left in the show, we would finally talk football.

Some of Merritt's descriptive terms were priceless. "Quick as a hiccup," he would say, describing the speed of a particular player. Or "Flip the light switch, and he'll be in bed before it's dark." And, a favorite, "The hay's in the barn, baby," meaning all the work has been done, and it's time to play the game.

One final note about the *John Merritt Show*. He did two commercials during each show. One was for Bunny Bread, and the other was for a furniture company that provided him with the recliner he used on the set (and one at home, of course). When it was time for John to talk about his sponsor he would pull the lever on the side of the chair, lean back, take a long draw on his cigar, let the smoke slowly escape, and launch into how that recliner had cured his back problems, enabling him to sleep like a baby at night. The man was a natural born showman.

## ❖ What's for Supper?

I got a phone call late one Friday afternoon from John. He called to invite me to his house that night for, as he put it, "A gathering of friends for supper."

I arrived at his house shortly after my six o'clock sportscast and was greeted by his lovely and gracious wife, Maxine. As I stepped inside, I heard voices and laughter and smelled an aroma I didn't recognize. She led me to the den, where Big John was holding court.

The cigar smoke was already hanging heavy, and John was in the middle of telling a very funny story. He saw me, winked, and kept talking and entertaining. And then I saw him: seated on the couch across from John, laughing as hard as anybody in the room, was Eddie Robinson. Yes, *the* Eddie Robinson, legendary head coach of Grambling University, Tennessee State's opponent the next day in the "Hole." I chuckled to myself as I tried to process what I was seeing.

There were John Merritt and Eddie Robinson, two long-time rival head coaches of two of the largest predominantly black universities in the nation. They had gathered with members of their coaching staffs on the evening before their biggest game of the year for some fun and relaxation.

I had done a sit-down interview with Eddie Robinson earlier that day, and we talked about their relationship as coaches, and their admiration for each other. But in my wildest thoughts I could never have imagined joining him for supper that evening.

His story completed, John turned to me and said, "Hope, you know Eddie Robinson," and then he introduced Eddie's assistant coaches.

Maxine told the gathering it was time for supper. John said the blessing (he could just as easily have been a preacher too) and said, "Hope I want you to lead us off in line."

I picked up my plate and started toward the buffet. That's when the unfamiliar aroma became the strongest, as my nostrils flared from the scent. John draped his arm around my shoulders, leaned down, and said, "How do you like your . . . chitlins? Hot sauce, or plain?" The room erupted with laughter. "I gotta warn you," Merritt teased, "eat a plate of those chitlins, and about three a.m. the toilet's gonna be your best friend. You'll be doing the 'chitlin strut' from the bedroom to the bathroom." Laughter erupted again.

I tried to eat some chitlins but quickly discovered they are not for the faint of palate or smell. In case you're wondering . . . yes, it was my first—and my last—chitlin party.

### ❖ Eating Crow

One year during football season, I predicted Tennessee State would lose to a certain opponent, but the Tigers ended up winning by several touchdowns. The following Monday at six, as I was delivering the sports, Merritt walked into the studio (with the knowledge of everyone but me) and placed on the set in front of me a silver platter with a dead crow on it. He then handed me a rather large fork and said I should eat a little crow for picking TSU to lose that weekend. Of course, everyone in the studio and control room broke up laughing, as well as, I'm sure, all the viewers at home. Big John had his revenge.

By now you have gathered that John Merritt and I had become good friends, and because of that I broke my rule. I always tried really hard to make it a practice never to become friends with the people I had to cover as a reporter. Friendship could very easily prevent you from reporting on that person or team in an honest and non-biased manner. I broke that rule with John, because . . . well, because he was John Merritt, one of the most engaging, charismatic, lovable guys I have ever had the pleasure of knowing.

### ❖ Show Me the Money

The creative mind of John Merritt never ceased to amaze me. He called one day and asked if I would go on a short in-home recruiting trip with him. He picked me up in his Cadillac, freshly detailed and glimmering. John said he needed to stop by the bank on the way out of town, so we did. The young man John was recruiting lived in Cookeville. We arrived late in the afternoon and spent well over an hour visiting with the player, his mother, several brothers and sisters, a grandmother, several aunts, and a few cousins. John's performance was spellbinding, but the young man was being highly recruited by several schools, and John needed a closer. Something dramatic that would impress the player and everyone else who had come to hear Big John give his pitch.

"Well, everybody, I want to thank you for your hospitality. It's been a wonderful opportunity getting to know all of you, but now it's time for us to be getting back to Nashville," John said, as he lifted himself off the couch.

He reached in his pants pocket and extracted a wad of money wrapped with several rubber bands, a hundred dollar bill clearly visible on the outside. "Hope, we need to get some gas and something to eat on our way out of town." After making sure everyone in the room had seen his stash of green, he placed the money in his other pants pocket and smiled.

"Just want you all to know that Big John takes care of all his boys. Whatever they need, I see they get it."

That was one proud mama when her son signed with Tennessee State.

## ❖ One Man's Gift

John Merritt was tremendously gifted with personality and wit. He could make you feel like a million dollars, because he loved people. All people. He loved giving, and he gave abundantly of himself. John also knew his limitations. That's why he always surrounded himself with people smarter than he was. He could certainly motivate his players with a rousing pre-game or half-time speech. He could raise money for his program with the best of them, and he would out-recruit you before sundown. But when it came to the Xs and Os of football, John hired men smarter and more capable of teaching the fundamentals of the game than he was. And he gave them credit, singing their praises for any success achieved. That, I believe, was his genius.

In addition to television, my early years in Nashville included a stint on the radio. I mentioned earlier that I would tell the story of how Larry Munson helped me land a football play-by-play job on a fifty-thousand-watt radio station. That station was WLAC in Nashville. Management decided they would broadcast several Tennessee State games one year and began looking for someone to handle the play-by-play duties. The station manager was a good friend of Munson's and asked him to recommend someone for the job. Larry was familiar with my work in Athens and recommended me. I did five or six home games that season, and that experience would pay huge dividends when I got to San Diego one year later.

## ❖ Put Me In, Coach

I've involved myself in some rather questionable endeavors over the years, and this one was one of the more dubious. Twenty-nine-year-old Steve Sloan became head coach of the Vanderbilt football team in 1973, and he put together an impressive staff to say the least. Bill Parcells was the defensive coordinator. Rex Dockery (who was later killed in a plane crash in 1983 while head coach at Memphis State) was Sloan's offensive coordinator. George MacIntyre, later to become head coach at Vandy, coached defensive backs.

George Plimpton wrote his classic, *Paper Lion*, about his experiences going through training camp with the 1963 Detroit Lions. I figured if Plimpton could do it, so could I. So in 1973, I decided to go out for spring pracice with the Vanderbilt football team (pads and all), film it, and show the highlights on the six and ten o'clock news. What was I thinking?

I talked to Coach Sloan about my idea, and he loved it. We decided I should play fullback, and like Barney Fife on the *Andy Griffith Show*, who had only one bullet, coach Sloan gave me only one play to learn: fullback smash over center.

I reported to the Vanderbilt equipment room and was issued pads, shoes, a helmet, and a uniform. I got some pretty intense stares from players in the locker room, and those stares turned into snickers when I was handed my jersey: my number was "double zero."

The first few practices went fairly well. Of course, I wasn't in the same physical condition the Vandy players were by any stretch

In Hines' Sight

of the imagination, so you could say I struggled. Oh, you could definitely say I struggled. And they didn't take it easy on me—in fact, it was just the opposite. During team drills, the coaches yelled and poked fun at me as I attempted to keep up. I did everything the running backs did except take part in live scrimmages. Coach Sloan said I would be given one, and only one, opportunity to carry the ball. It would come sometime near the end of the annual Black and Gold Game in the spring.

I had been practicing with the team for about two weeks (three times a week) when, to my great surprise, Coach Sloan stopped practice one afternoon and motioned for me to join the offense. It was one of those *you talking to me?* moments. I hustled over to the offensive huddle, where Sloan was standing. He placed his hand on my shoulder pads as I strapped on my chin strap. "Hope," he began, "I've decided you need to carry the ball one time before the spring game to get you ready." Now, this was a live scrimmage, mind you, and when Sloan spoke, my knees got a little weak. Make that a whole lot weak.

It wasn't complicated. All I had to do was line up behind center at fullback. Quarterback Fred Fisher would hand me the ball, and I would run straight ahead, behind an offensive line I knew wanted to make me look good.

We huddled up. Fred said, "Fullback smash. Zero dive. On two." We clapped and broke huddle. My heart was pounding as several of the defensive players shouted remarks in my direction that were not what I would call endearing. But I would show them. Show them that I had what it takes . . . whatever that was.

I went down in my fullback three-point stance. I was tense, but I was ready. My last thought was, "That damn camera better be rolling, cause I might not live through this."

The ball was snapped. Fred turned and stuck it in my gut. As I lunged toward center, I knew I was going to get hit, and hit hard. I winced, waiting for the eleven-body pileup that was about to happen, when suddenly the line in front of me parted like the Red Sea. I fell head first into the turf, rolling over and over until I came to a sudden stop. Not a single player had touched me.

It had been the bright idea of defensive coordinator Bill Parcells, who had persuaded Coach Sloan they should have some fun at my expense. Parcells had told both the offensive and defensive linemen to part and leave a huge hole for me to stumble through on the snap of the ball. It worked perfectly.

My own momentum, created by leaning forward in anticipation of being tackled, had caused me to fall on my face. I looked around through the ear-hole of my helmet and could see players, coaches, and sideline onlookers doubled over with laughter.

Parcells later became a Super Bowl–winning coach, and our paths have crossed several times over the years. Each time we met he would smile and say, "Keeping your head up?"

Oh, yeah. The Black and Gold game. Well, I did play. One play, and one play only. I was on the Black team. There were less than two minutes left in the game. We were inside the Gold's five-yard line. Sloan called time out, called me off the bench, and said, "This is it, Hope. You know the play. Do not fumble."

As I ran onto the field, the PA announcer told the crowd, "Double zero, Hope Hines, in at fullback." Of course the whole stadium knew who would get the ball. Channel 5 photographer Fred Skipworth was there to record the play, which would be shown on the ten o'clock news that night. I was ready. This would be a moment to tell my grandchildren about.

We lined up. The ball was snapped. The quarterback turned and handed it to me. I was immediately hit, and . . . do I really have to tell you what happened?

Okay! I fumbled. The Gold team recovered, and that's all I'm gonna say about that.

## ❖ A Star Is Born

She appeared one day in the Channel 5 newsroom. I noticed nothing especially outstanding about her, except that she was black and very young, with a certain undefined quality. Her personality was warm and infectious. I recall how poised she was for someone so young, and there was something else: she loved to talk. To anyone, about anything.

Those were my first impressions of Oprah Winfrey.

Chris Clark hired Oprah as a reporter in 1973. She was a nineteen-year-old sophomore at Tennessee State University. With apparent magical talent for television, Oprah soon became both the youngest news anchor and the first black female news anchor in Nashville.

Oprah tells a revealing story of her early days as an anchor on her website. In an attempt to look like her 1970s idol, Mary Tyler Moore, she tied scarves around her neck and wore false eyelashes that she bought at Walgreens. "I didn't know how to put them on very well," she says. "By the end of the newscast, my eyelash would be coming off."

My wife, Pat, remembers meeting Oprah thirty-nine years ago in the Channel 5 newsroom. She says she was immediately captivated by her persona. She even remembers how genuinely complementary Oprah was about Pat's outfit, and Pat has never forgotten exactly what she wore that evening. My wife has told that story many times over the years, because it's an example of Oprah's extraordinary talent for making others feel special.

Oprah and I would cross career paths again a few years later after we both left Channel 5. I'll tell you how we walked the streets of Baltimore together in a later chapter.

## ❖ Off to See the Greatest

Lon Varnell was one of the most fascinating people I have ever encountered—a Nashville promoter extraordinaire, and so much more. Lon was a three-sport athlete at Freed-Hardeman College. Following graduation, he coached high school basketball. An innovative coach, he is credited with first using the hook shot and the 2–3 zone defense. In 1944, Adolph Rupp invited Varnell to assist him at Kentucky, where he helped recruit the "Fabulous Five."

Then in 1948, Varnell was hired as head basketball coach at the University of the South in Sewanee, Tennessee. Coach Rupp recommended him for the job, saying, "Next to me, Lon Varnell is the best coach in America."

Varnell also began working with the Harlem Globetrotters as a promoter; he helped open the South to their performances. Lon established Lon Varnell Enterprises in Nashville; his company promoted everything from country acts to Lawrence Welk concerts.

*Sports Illustrated* paid tribute to Varnell in February 1969, calling him a "legend in his own time. A coach, a Methodist minister, coal mine operator, car dealer, political campaign manager, hardware store owner, and promoter of entertainment."

In the fall of 1974, I got a call from Lon asking if we could have lunch. He had an idea he wanted to discuss with me. Of course I agreed. Lon said he had the theater rights across the South to promote the upcoming Muhammad Ali–George Foreman heavyweight fight in Kinshasa, Zaire. The fight, known as "The Rumble in the Jungle," was scheduled for October 30. Lon's proposal was this: a photographer and I would go to Zaire several weeks before the fight, conduct interviews with Ali and Foreman, and shoot lots of film of the two fighters as they prepared. I would bring the film back before the fight so that Lon could use the footage to promote the fight in his theaters.

Lon said he would finance 50 percent of the trip if Channel 5 would pick up the other 50 percent. It was the genius of Lon Varnell at work. I couldn't wait to meet with my bosses to get their reaction, although I was highly skeptical they would agree.

To my utter amazement, they said yes. Lon would get what he wanted, and Channel 5 would have film that no other local station in the country would have. Wow! What a deal.

Channel 5 photographer Milton McClurken and I flew to New York, where we were processed as members of the media, and from there we traveled to Kinshasa, Zaire, for an unbelievable adventure of a lifetime.

A disturbing sight greeted us on arrival at the Kinshasa airport. Military police were everywhere. We were searched, and our bags were opened for inspection. When they discovered our camera and equipment, we were detained, even though we displayed all the proper media credentials. After several hours of waiting, we were finally interrogated and cleared to leave the airport. I remember telling Milton, "If we lose our credentials, we will be in a world (third world) of hurt."

The hotel where the media was assigned had no air conditioning, and the rooms were small by American standards, with one small bed. I recall looking out my hotel window in late afternoon to the streets below, and seeing people hurrying along. Kinshasa was then a city of several million people located on the Congo River. I looked out my window again later that night just before going to bed. The scene was completely different. There on the streets were entire families sleeping on cardboard. It was a heart-breaking sight.

Joseph Mobutu was the self-proclaimed dictator of Zaire, and for the next several days we boarded a bus each morning that took us to Mobutu's compound along the Congo River, where Ali and Foreman trained. Each day, schoolchildren were brought to the training center to watch Ali. At the end of his workout, he would sit with the children and sing songs. Their favorite chant was, "Ali Boom Mah Yea! Ali Boom Mah Yea!" Translated it means, "Ali Kill Him." George Foreman was not the people's choice, and he refused to talk with the media the entire time he was training.

My first interview with Ali was to follow one of the afternoon sessions as soon as his visit with the children was over. I introduced myself to his trainer, Angelo Dundee, who approved all interviews, and we hit it off right away.

We were the only camera crew in Kinshasa for the first few days, and Ali couldn't have been more accommodating. In fact he was starved for some on-camera attention and was just as terrific as advertised.

Lunch was provided each day for the media and invited special guests. One day, Dundee invited me to sit with him and suggested that I let him order for me. When my lunch was served, Angelo went into this long explanation of how the food was superbly prepared with special ingredients, and he was certain it would fit in quite nicely with the Southern cuisine I was accustomed to. The large mound of food on my plate looked inviting. The taste was . . . well, like nothing I had ever experienced, but not terrible. About midway through the meal, Angelo casually asked me how I was enjoying my specially prepared dish of . . . monkey. Ever since then, guess which part of the zoo I bypass.

But all in all it was a wonderful experience, except for the armed military that walked the streets of Kinshasa. They often seemed to forget that they were the hosts and we, the members of the media, were their invited guests. Mobutu certainly wanted the attention his country would get from the fight, but his military was not accustomed to a free press, which made it difficult for us to do our jobs on many occasions.

Arriving at the Kinshasa airport for our return trip to Nashville, we were once again detained and searched. The officer in charge said our baggage was overweight and we would have to pay something like three hundred dollars before we could board. I looked at Milton in disbelief. Between us we had maybe seventy-five dollars in Zaire money. We tried to reason with the officer, but to no avail. Just then, another officer—witnessing our dilemma—came over and spoke to the first officer. His mannerisms and tone told us he was a high-ranking official, and he was not pleased with his subordinate's handling of our luggage. He politely turned to us, apologized for the unfortunate incident, and told us we were free to board our flight.

On board, Milton and I breathed a heavy sigh of relief, with thoughts of "home sweet home," as the plane gently lifted off into the late afternoon African sky. Destination . . . Music City.

## In Hines' Sight

My trip to Kinshasa in 1974 was an invaluable learning experience that I have never forgotten. What promoter Lon Varnell did is now called thinking outside the box. He came up with a creative way to solve his problem of promoting the Ali-Foreman fight in theaters across the Southeast.

That experience has been one of the great influences in my life and career, and I have reflected upon it many times when trying to solve a problem.

In order to think outside the box, we must first understand what the box is. Then we can begin to maneuver outside, over, and around the box.

There's nothing mystical about the box. To the contrary; the box is the normal, everyday way we see things, which restricts our thinking and beliefs. The box is our comfort zone, but it is also a self-imposed prison of convictions. For us to break out, we must challenge all things that cause us to think inside those walls. That's exactly what Lon Varnell did when he went outside the normal channels of doing business.

Varnell had a lot in common with Muhammad Ali himself. They both thought differently than most. You might say they both achieved more than most by thinking outside the box. Although with Ali it was a case of thinking outside the . . . ring.

In the history of sport, there has never been anyone like Ali. Observing this great boxer up close in Kinshasa those few days, I witnessed his flair for the dramatic up close. He loved the sport of boxing. Perhaps even more than that, however, he adored the attention. He had a highly developed aptitude for oration, and he loved people.

I was fortunate enough to have covered Ali on several other occasions, both in the ring and in other settings. His persona always comes to mind when I lack the confidence to perform certain endeavors. If we all could muster just a portion of what drove Ali, think what any of us could achieve with our lives.

## ❖ Skywriters

We were men from towns and cities all across the Southeast, respected in our communities and loved by our families, but when we boarded that chartered Southern Airways DC-3 every August in Birmingham, Alabama, we immediately transformed into a fraternity of dysfunctional journalists. Blaming it on the hospitality of our hosts, you could have accurately described us as the original "boys gone wild."

Our little band of scribes and TV sportscasters were forty members of the SEC Skywriters tour. It was our job (we would have gladly paid for the privilege) to travel to all ten of the conference schools and report on fall football practice.

My longtime friend Roy Exum, who then wrote for the *Chattanooga News-Free Press*, summed up our yearly escapades with this account:

> Once I was in Knoxville and Ben Byrd, the longtime editor of the *Journal*, walked up and said in his staid way, "I hear they want to write a book on the Skywriters, so get ready, we've got to pay whatever it takes to squelch it.

The Skywriters tour lasted from 1965 to 1983, under the direction—and sometimes misdirection—of the late Elmore "Scoop" Hudgins, the legendary and much-beloved SEC media relations director.

When we boarded the DC-3 each year, the late Jack Hairston, longtime editor of the *Gainesville Sun* and our self-proclaimed tour director, would commandeer the PA as the plane was taxiing down the runway. He would then read horrid accounts of plane crashes he had gathered during the year. That's when many of our travelers would reach for their companions, Jack Daniels and Jim Beam. When the plane was airborne, Hairston would launch into what amounted to a roast of various writers he chose to pick on. Before the trip ended, we would all be fodder for Hairston's sharp tongue and quick wit.

Each school we visited during our ten-day ordeal—I mean, trip—hosted a dinner party with free food and booze. These parties always lasted into the early-morning hours. One year, Scoop Hudgins tried to initiate the buddy system for accountability. There were several occasions following one of these all-nighters when members of our group never made takeoff and were left behind. Can you imagine trying to get a flight from Starkville to Auburn . . . in one day?

Ron Higgins, writing for *SEC Traditions*:

"Among those who didn't mind having a good time was the plane's pilot, who we nicknamed Crash. The night before the start of the tour one year, most of us were playing cards and drinking till 2 or 3 in the morning," said Mike McKenzie, former sports editor of the *Advocate* in Baton Rouge. "And there's this guy with us all night, just laughing and having a great time. We didn't know who he was, and nobody asked him. We boarded the plane the next morning and the guy is already on board. He's the PILOT."

Longtime *Tennessean* sports writer Jimmy Davy, now retired, says, "Crash often left the cabin door open, so we could see right into the cockpit. One morning we're all getting on the plane in Oxford and we look up in the cockpit. There's Crash laid back in his seat . . . wearing an oxygen mask."

Some of the Skywriters are now deceased, and many are retired, but some continue to work. Over a thousand print, Internet, radio, and TV journalists, many of whom are blogging and tweeting their messages, attend the media days in Birmingham now. But

I wonder how many of today's breed could have endured the hardships of a Skywriter in those days of typewriters and twenty-hour work days (okay, we worked maybe two, but we were *up* for twenty hours). Again, to quote my friend Roy Exum, "Too many would fall prey to demon rum, outlandish behavior, a roller-coaster ride, and the most merriment that could be shoe-horned into any twenty-four-hour day."

Long live the SEC Skywriters.

Hey, I just had a thought: how about a Skywriters Senior Tour? I wonder whatever happened to Crash?

---

## In Hines' Sight

You might ask: what did I learn from all those years as a member of the Skywriters tour? Nothing! I already knew how to have a good time.

### ❖ The Masters Experience (With Humor)

My first visit to the Masters golf tournament had been while working in radio in Athens, Georgia. As sports director, I received two press badges each spring, and I eagerly awaited the month of April each year.

The first time I walked onto the hallowed grounds of Augusta National, I felt as if I were strolling through an earthly garden of Eden. It was breathtaking, and I began to understand what the experience of the Masters was all about.

I recall going to the Masters in 1969 with Georgia All-American defensive tackle Bill Stanfill. Bill was drafted in the first round by the Miami Dolphins that year and went on to become a four-time first team all-pro and played for the Dolphins during their 1972 undefeated season, including their Super Bowl victory over the Redskins. We drove Bill's car . . . actually I drove his car while Bill's six-foot-five, 250-pound frame somehow soaked up what must have been a case of beer. Not to mention all the Georgia fans who recognized Bill and bought him cup after cup of beer. It was a quiet ride home to Athens that night, except for Bill's snoring in the back seat.

The previous year, I had taken Bill home to Quitman, where he spoke at the Brooks County football banquet. We spent the night with my parents, and the next morning mother opened the bedroom door to get us up. Bill and I were sleeping in twin beds, and when she saw Bill's legs hanging over the end of the bed she burst out laughing. Our beds were not built for a six-foot-five-inch body, and mother thought it was one of the funniest sights she had ever seen. She told that story many times over the years to family and friends.

Many years later, while covering the Masters in 1980, I interviewed the 1979 winner Fuzzy Zoeller, who is one of three golfers to have won the Masters in their first appearance. I asked Fuzzy what his first impressions of the course were the year before. "If there is a golf course in heaven," Fuzzy quickly responded, "it surely will look just like Augusta National."

My good fortune of being able to cover the Masters continued while I was at Channel 5 during the '70s. Each year I would go to Augusta and conduct interviews during the practice rounds, then I would return and air those interviews later in the week during the six o'clock and ten o'clock news. So popular was the Masters footage that I would often be invited to speak and show the interviews on a projector at various Middle Tennessee civic groups.

In those days, I was one of a handful of TV reporters covering the Masters, and getting interviews with the stars of the game, like Arnold Palmer, Jack Nicklaus, Gary Player, and Johnny Miller, was not difficult. We would set up our camera under the Big Oak Tree, which shades the clubhouse on the golf course side, and wait for the golfers to complete their rounds. We would then grab them on their way inside. The Masters was also where I forged friendships with Nashville's Lou Graham and Mason Rudolph.

One of the highlights of my career happened during one of those practice rounds at Augusta. Lee Trevino had been one of the hottest golfers on tour in the early and mid 1970s, winning a U.S. Open, two British Opens, and a PGA Championship. He was also one of the funniest and most approachable golfers on the tour. In those days, the rules for TV crews on the course during practice rounds were fairly lax. My photographer, Fred Skipworth, and I had followed Trevino for several holes. We were shooting footage from just outside the ropes when he hit a shot that landed just a few feet from where we were filming.

*Left:* My 1960 high school senior football picture.
*Above:* With my brothers Morris and Tom and parents Floreine and Lyman at Tom's wedding in 1978.

WLAC-TV weatherman Bob Lobertini, news anchor Chris Clark, and me, 1972.

With the late John Merritt, Tennessee State head football coach, 1972.

Riding a bull at the Loretta Lynn rodeo in Nashville 1973—I lasted a whopping two seconds.

Two legends of golf at the 1972 Masters: Arnold Palmer (above) and Jack Nicklaus (right).

With Pat at the 1975 Masters.

Evangelist Billy
Graham on set in San
Diego with Dick
Carlson, Barney
Morris, and me, 1976.

With Padres pitcher
Randy Jones and
Chargers
quarterback Dan
Fouts at the Andy
Williams San Diego
Open, 1976.

Speaking at a luncheon in San Diego honoring McDonald's founder Ray Kroc, 1977. Actor and television producer Danny Thomas is standing to my my right.

With Chargers receiver Lance Alworth and George Pernicano, minority owner of the Chargers, 1977.

Walking the picket line in Baltimore 1982 during strike of on air WMAR-TV AFTRA members.

Cover of *Nashville!* magazine, 1985. With Charlie McAlexander, Channel 4, and Bob Bell, Channel 2.

*Left:* With Phillip Fulmer, University of Tennessee Head Football coach, early 1990s. *Above:* With legendary University of Tennessee women's basketball coach Pat Summitt, late 1980s.

*Left:* Reporting from the 1986 Sugar Bowl, Tennessee vs. Miami. *Below:* With good friend Lewis Grizzard at his home in Atlanta, New Year's eve 1987. *Bottom left:* CBS *Late Show* host David Letterman, 1990. *Bottom right:* George Foreman, former World Heavyweight boxing champion, early 1990s.

*Clockwise from top left:* My wife Pat posing with University of Tennessee quarterback Peyton Manning at the 1996 Florida Citrus Bowl in Orlando; Christmas 1994, with Pat at Thornburry Castle, England; good friend Jimmy Hampton with me and Pat at a pub in London; Pat ready for dinner at Thornburry Castle.

With Pat and Governor Don Sundquist of Tennessee in 2001. I was honored to be asked to speak at the Governor's Prayer Breakfast.

*Above:* Legendary country music entertainer Jerry Reed, my son Danny, Nascar Hall of Famer Darrell Waltrip, and others. *Right:* With my son Lyman at the World Series, Atlanta, 1992.

He walked over to his ball and noticed that Fred was shooting. "That thing got color film?" Trevino blurted out, followed by a silly laugh.

"Yes, sir, it does," I responded.

Trevino tore into the ball, and it landed just short of the green. "That ball's got lead in it. Think I'll give it to Jack." (Jack Nicklaus was Trevino's chief rival in the '70s.)

Trevino then dropped another ball (remember, this was a practice round) and flew it to within three feet of the pin. "Did you get that?" he said, looking at Fred, who gave him a thumbs-up from behind the camera.

Trevino then turned to me and said, "What's your name, young man?"

"Hope Hines, from Nashville, Tennessee," I said.

"Tell Johnny Cash 'The Merry Mex' said hello," Trevino responded. Then he motioned for us to follow him on the course.

"I don't think we're allowed inside the ropes," I said.

"Unless you see Clifford Roberts [chairman of Augusta National Golf Club] standing behind a tree, come on."

I interviewed Trevino as we walked to the green. It was one of the funniest dialogues I have ever been a part of. I learned that Augusta National was not one of Trevino's favorite courses. He felt he didn't belong there, and he asked officials every year not to invite him back. During that walking interview, he had some very critical—but humorous—things to say about the course and about the fact that he was a minority playing at an exclusive "white man's club." He disliked the club so much that he changed his shoes in the parking lot. It was his own personal protest.

## In Hines' Sight

The Masters served as another opportunity for me to observe the best players in the world perform with incredible accuracy. The advantage of observing the best at anything is invaluable. When we find ourselves in such an arena, we must closely observe what they do and how they do it. In sports, in business, in social settings, wherever you find the best . . . never be afraid to copy them.

### ❖ Clowning Around

Twice a year during the '70s, the TV show *Hee Haw* was taped at WLAC-TV (now WTVF). The show aired on CBS from 1969 through 1971, before a twenty-year run in national syndication. Cohosted by Buck Owens and Roy Clark, with a cornfield backdrop, the show was centered around country music. It featured lots of comedy and musical talent, plus voluptuous, scantily clad women who were known as the "Hee Haw Honeys."

The show's producer, Sam Lovullo, was a huge sports fan. Each year he would bring in high-profile athletes, usually baseball and PGA tour players, to make guest appearances. Almost every year, Hall of Fame catcher Johnny Bench of the Cincinnati Reds would be a guest. I struck up a friendship with Johnny, one we have maintained over the years. One year Johnny shot several TV promo spots on my behalf that ran during baseball playoff season. What a thrill that was for me. Hall of Fame pitcher Dizzy Dean was also a yearly guest on *Hee Haw*. Hanging out with Bench and Dean were certainly highlights of the year for me.

During the weeks when *Hee Haw* was taping, you never knew who you would run into in the hallway on the second level at Channel 5. One day, the elevator doors opened and out stepped Academy Award–winning actor Ernest Borgnine . . . in overalls.

Lecile Harris was a talented rodeo clown. He was named rodeo clown of the year four times. He was also a session drummer at the now famous Memphis Sun Studio and an actor as well. Lecile became a regular on *Hee Haw* in the early '70s, and we became friends. The Loretta Lynn Rodeo was playing at the downtown Municipal Arena one October, and Lecile was one of the clowns. We were talking on the *Hee Haw* set one day, and out of the blue he said, "Hope, why don't you ride a bull in the rodeo on Saturday night? Have your photographer film it, and show it on the ten o'clock news. It'll be a great promotional stunt."

"You've got to be kidding," I replied.

"Look," he continued, "we won't put you on the meanest, baddest bull, and besides I'll be in the ring with you every step of the way. Just think about it. Besides you're not gonna stay on long enough to get hurt, and the crowd will love it, I promise you."

"Yeah," I said, "but it's not *your* butt sitting on that bull."

I talked to station management, and they agreed that it could be a nice promotional piece, but the decision was mine.

I talked to Lecile again. We agreed I would go over to the arena the next day and check things out. He wanted me to sit on a bull, in the closely confined pen they use, to get the feel of it. I did, and after some coaxing from Lecile and several other cowboys . . . I said okay.

Several days before the Saturday ride, I began promoting it on the six and ten o'clock news, telling the audience what I planned to do. I got several phone calls over the next few days from people saying, in one way or another, they wouldn't miss it, because they wanted to see my "smart ass" flying through the air. I couldn't back out now.

And I didn't disappoint them. That October Saturday at Nashville's Municipal Arena is forever etched in my memory. The rodeo PA announcer had been telling the audience all evening I would be riding a bull later, and they were ready to see blood. Mine.

At the appointed time, I gently eased onto the back of a two-thousand-pound animal who was not in a good mood. He kept snorting and banging against the sides of the chute. Lecile was talking to me, trying to calm my nerves. Family moments kept flashing through my mind. Would I ever see my children again? Then I was instructed to place my gloved left hand, palm up, under the rope on the bull's back so they could tie what the cowboys call the "death wrap." Oh, what fun. They placed another rope on top of my hand and pulled it so tight I had no feeling in my fingers. Lecile looked at me. He later told me that at that moment I had the look of a man on death row.

"Are you ready?" he said. I tried to answer, but nothing came out. Then someone shouted, "Let 'er go!"

The gate swung open. My brain was frozen, but my heart was pounding. The bull snorted and lunged out of the chute. I was still on. Then came a wild series of bucks, jumps, and kicks, and to the delight of the crowd, I was now airborne. I don't remember a thing except slamming hard into the wire fence. Lecile was quick to divert the bull's attention away from me, and I was assisted by several other clowns to safety. My reward was a standing ovation from the crowd, and the knowledge that I rode a bull for . . . two whole seconds. That's gotta be a record for a "fool" sportscaster.

The following week, Loretta Lynn had a pair of mounted "Texas cow" horns delivered to Channel 5 and presented them to me on the set of the six o'clock news. It was a wonderful gesture, and I kept those "long horns" for years as a reminder of one of the dumbest things I ever did in my life.

## ❖ Another King and I

After my first few years of television in Nashville, I fancied myself as somewhat of a hot shot. I liked doing the offbeat things that would flabbergast and astonish the audience—like the Vanderbilt football game and riding a bull. On occasions I purposely did commentaries that would incite and agitate viewers.

Then came the Billie Jean King incident in 1973. Billie Jean had dominated women's tennis for nearly two decades.

She was in Nashville to participate in the Virginia Slims of Nashville tournament, where she faced Margaret Court in the finals at the Centennial Tennis Center. King lost to Court, her longtime rival, for the third time in four matches.

I was there with my photographer to cover the match, and when it was over, tournament officials informed us that Billie Jean would not be talking with the media.

For whatever reason, I took her refusal to speak with the media personally and felt she was acting like a bad sport, not to mention that it seemed like a slap in the face to the Nashville media not to talk just because she lost. So I told my photographer that we were going to station ourselves outside the door to the ladies dressing room and wait for King to come out. I told him to roll the camera and not to turn it off for any reason. I intended to ambush her. We had been standing there about fifteen minutes when suddenly the door opened and immediately slammed shut. Whoever opened the door obviously saw me standing there with a camera and closed it with a loud bang.

Another fifteen or so minutes went by. I made certain the camera continued to roll, because whatever happened I was going to show it on the six o'clock news. Suddenly, the door opened. There were at least three people making a wedge and running interference for Ms. King as they rushed out the door.

In Hines' Sight

I quickly stepped in front of Billie Jean and shoved the microphone in her face, badgering her with questions about why she refused to talk to the media. She was startled and didn't quite know how she wanted to react to this "male chauvinist punk" who apparently thought he was Mike Wallace of *60 Minutes*. When she regained her composure, she blurted out, "Who do you think you are? I don't have to answer any of your questions. Now would you get out of my way, I have a plane to catch."

That's not true, Ms. King," I said. I had already checked on her plane reservations, and I knew that in fact she was not scheduled to fly out until almost three hours later. She looked at me in utter disbelief. "How dare you call me a liar."

"Are you in fact leaving for the airport now?" I questioned.

"That's none of your business."

I continued my questioning. "Would you just answer why you refuse to speak with anybody in the Nashville media?"

Then, in a loud, irritated voice, she said to no one in particular, "Somebody get an official over here . . . NOW."

I knew when to quit. I motioned to my camera man, and we walked away. I had what I wanted, the entire episode on film. That night middle Tennessee viewers saw my hostile attempt to interview Billie Jean King. To some I was definitely the bad guy, and I was. A few applauded my efforts. Whatever the case, it made for some really good TV, and folks talked about it for some time.

## ❖ A Helping Hand

The phone rang in my office at Channel 5 one day, and on the other end was a familiar and favorite voice. Harry Chapman was calling from Atlanta. Harry and I had worked together several years at WGAU in Athens while we both went to journalism school. Harry graduated before I did and was working at WSB radio in Atlanta as a DJ. He was calling to ask if there might be any openings for a news reporter at Channel 5. I told him I would talk with our news director Chris Clark and get back to him.

I spoke to Chris and highly recommended Harry, who was invited for an interview and eventually got the job. Harry is one of my favorite people. He likes to tell everyone I am responsible for his coming to Nashville, but the truth is that Harry got the job because of his talent. He and Oprah Winfrey coanchored the weekend news for several years. Later, he was a cohost on *Talk of the Town*. Harry was a popular personality on Channel 5 for many, many years. His talent was versatile, and he did an excellent job covering Nashville's music industry.

### ❖ When You're Hot, You're Hot

I met Jerry Reed one summer morning at Fate Sanders boat dock on Percy Priest Lake. Jerry had been on the lake until just after sun-up, night fishing for bass. He was having breakfast, and he was the center of attention, telling everyone about his night on Priest and his catch.

Jerry, who never met a stranger, recognized me from the news when I walked into the boat dock restaurant.

"Hope Hines, come over here and sit down. I'm gonna buy you breakfast, 'cause I want you to go back and tell everybody on TV not only can Ole Jerry sing a tune or two and play a little guitar, he's one fine fisherman." He laughed and slapped me on the back as I settled into the seat next to him.

That was my introduction to "The Guitar Man," entertainer extraordinaire, singer, songwriter, and actor. It was also the beginning of a dear friendship that lasted until Jerry's death in 2008.

Jerry loved night fishing, and many times I would meet him after the ten o'clock news at the lake for some all-night fishing and howling. Jerry had a custom-built red, white, and blue bass boat with an out-of-this-world sound system.

Jerry would crank up his 1971 monster hit "When You're Hot, You're Hot," and we'd head off into the night, screaming across the lake at speeds I don't even want to think about.

Through my friendship with Jerry, I had the pleasure of meeting many wonderful session players and producers. We both loved golf, and our foursome at times included Chet Atkins, Glen Campbell, Mac Davis, and others.

### ❖ Sports Trivia at the Big Nickel

In 1971, there was a young songwriter and singer who worked at Channel 5 as a handyman. I would see this guy in the hallways of the station, whistling and singing to himself, just as happy as he could be. He introduced himself to me one day this way: "Hi, I'm Larry Gatlin. Betcha don't know where Dick Butkus went to college."

"Illinois," I shot back.

"Ray Nitschke?"

As I was thinking, he blurted out, "Illinois too. I need your job!" He laughed. After that, sports trivia became a game with us—we loved trying to stump each other. Larry's specialty was football. In the late '60s he had attended the University of Houston on a football scholarship.

One night about midnight I happened to look out the back door of my apartment in South Nashville, and who did I see across the yard sitting at his kitchen table strumming a guitar? It turned out that Larry and his wife, Janis, were my neighbors.

Larry's handyman career at Channel 5 didn't last very long. He would tell anyone who would listen that he was going to be a country music star. He was already performing in small clubs as a solo act while waiting on his brothers Steve and Rudy to finish college. During the '70s and '80s, Larry Gatlin and the Gatlin Brothers were among country music's most successful acts.

### ❖ A Time of Change

The mid 1970s brought tremendous change in my personal life. My wife Paula and I divorced, and later I married Pat, who had a son, Danny. We've been married almost forty years.

In the fall of 1975, I received a call from KFMB-TV, the CBS affiliate in San Diego, wanting to know if I would be interested in their sports position. I told them I would be happy to discuss the opening, and several phone calls led to an invitation to fly to the west coast for an interview.

Pat and I made our first trip to California, and we were very impressed with the station and the city of San Diego. Before we left to fly back to Nashville, they offered me the job. I said I would give them an answer in a few days. While there, I found out that in addition to the TV job I was interviewing for, the San Diego Chargers radio play-by-play job was open. I told station management I was interested in pursuing that job as well if I came to San Diego, and they encouraged me.

On the return trip home, Pat and I discussed the pros and cons of moving across country and leaving family and friends. The decision was not an easy one. It would mean leaving my daughter and son, who I would not see on a regular basis. It would also mean a totally different lifestyle.

We decided that even with our slight misgivings, the opportunity was just too good to pass up, and in December, just before Christmas, Pat, Danny, and I loaded up and headed for the west coast.

## In Hines' Sight

I figured leaving Nashville was either the best or the worst decision I ever made. Of course, I was counting on it being the best.

# West Coast Swing

## SAN DIEGO • 1975–1977

WE ARRIVED IN SAN DIEGO a few weeks before Christmas 1975 and settled in a house in Mira Mesa, then a large suburb of San Diego. Mira Mesa was bordered on the south by Miramar, the Unites States Navy Fighter Weapons School, more popularly known as "Top Gun."

The Chargers were scheduled to host the Jets on ABC's *Monday Night Football* on December 15, minus quarterback Joe Namath. Jets interim head coach Ken Shipp had benched Namath for a curfew violation, and the story was making national headlines. The Jets flew to town on Sunday before the Monday night game, and I interviewed Joe "Willie" at the team's hotel.

Namath had a cavalier attitude about the suspension; he laughed it off, saying it would make for some entertaining commentary from ABC's Howard Cosell.

There was a definite Nashville connection to that Monday night game at San Diego Stadium. John "J. J." Jones made his only NFL start that night, on the NFL's biggest stage, in place of Namath. Originally from Memphis, Jones had attended Fisk University. Jones played into the second quarter before Namath came off the bench. The Chargers won the game 24–16. Tragically Jones died in a house fire in University Place, West Virginia, in 2009.

### ❖ The View from Torrey Pines

February is PGA month in California, and it all began in 1976 with the Andy Williams San Diego Open at breathtaking Torrey Pines. Movie stars from L.A., athletes, and other notables were everywhere that week. I was invited to play in the Wednesday Pro-Am, and I didn't sleep a wink the night before. Thousands would be there to watch the pros and celebrities, and I knew my golf game wasn't ready for the inspection it was about to get. It turned out to be one of the highlights of my San Diego tour.

One of my broadcast idols, Vin Scully, the longtime voice of the Dodgers, was in the press tent one day, and I had the opportunity to visit with him. He was the perfect gentleman, not to mention the consummate broadcaster. He was genuinely interested in hearing about my career and background, and he invited me to join him in the Dodgers broadcast booth whenever I was in Los Angeles.

By the way, J. C. Snead, nephew of the legendary Sam Snead, won the tournament that year, making it back-to-back victories at Torrey Pines.

### ❖ Meeting a Cowboy Hero

Shortly after the San Diego Open, the Major League Baseball owners were holding their spring meeting in Phoenix. Padres president Buzzie Bavasi promised me that if I went to Phoenix and covered the meetings he would introduce me to my boyhood cowboy idol, Gene Autry, owner of the California Angels.

After landing in Phoenix, I arrived at the hotel and headed for the front desk. Suddenly, I heard Bavasi frantically calling my name across the lobby. He waved me over and said he would take me to meet Autry right away. We walked down a long corridor to a large banquet room, where the owners had just adjourned for lunch. Bavasi looked around, then he motioned for me to follow him into the men's restroom. Inside, several owners and executives were using the facilities—and there was Gene Autry, my boyhood cowboy idol, with his back to me . . . using the urinal.

While waiting for my introduction, my mind drifted back to my youth, and I recalled all of Gene's black and white movies, his wonder horse Champion, and his sidekicks Smiley Burnette and Pat Butram. Finally, Gene Autry, the only person to be awarded stars on the Hollywood Walk of Fame in five different categories (film, television, music, radio, and live performance) and the owner of the California Angels, turned and zipped up his pants.

We waited for him to wash and dry his hands. Then Buzzie Bavasi introduced me to Gene Autry.

I said something like, "I think I have seen all your pictures, Mr. Autry . . . you used to babysit me during the Saturday afternoon double feature at the movies."

"You and about ten million other kids," he said with a chuckle. "Where were you raised?" he asked.

"Georgia," I responded.

"Got lots of letters from youngsters in the South in those days. You ever write me a letter?"

"Yes sir, I did. I was about seven or eight, and I wrote asking if you would like to go on vacation with me and my family to Florida. You wrote me back to thank me for the invitation but said you were busy making movies and you couldn't leave Champion for that long. I kept that letter, Mr. Autry, for a number of years before it disappeared."

"Buzzie, take care of this young man. He's one of my boys." We shook hands. Later that day I couldn't wait to call my wife and tell her who I met in the men's restroom.

### ❖ Short-Order Cooks

The Padres were a Major League expansion team in 1969, and they languished at the bottom of the National League West each of their first six seasons. Team owner C. Arnholt Smith ran into financial trouble and almost moved the team to Washington, DC. At that point, Ray Kroc, the fast food visionary who founded McDonald's, entered the picture and paid ten million dollars for the team in 1974.

"I am not buying the Padres to make money," Kroc said. "I'm buying the Padres because I love baseball. The Padres will be my hobby."

Two months after Kroc bought the Padres, they opened the season at home against the Astros. The team was playing so badly that the feisty Kroc walked into the stadium announcer's booth, grabbed the public address microphone, and told the crowd, "I have never seen such stupid ball playing in my life."

After the game, *Sports Illustrated* quoted Astros third baseman Doug Rader, who said that Kroc should not treat his ballplayers like they were "short-order cooks."

The next time the Astros were in town, Kroc held a "Short-Order Cooks Night," with free admission for anyone wearing a chef's hat. That night Rader brought the lineup card to the plate wearing a chef's hat and apron and carrying a spatula. Kroc was so impressed that he later traded for Rader.

Kroc was passionate about the Padres, and he monitored the day-to-day operation of his team closely. He had his battles with Baseball Commissioner Bowie Kuhn. In fact, Kroc joined forces with such owners as Charlie Finley of the Oakland Athletics, Ted Turner of the Atlanta Braves, and George Steinbrenner of the New York Yankees for some well-documented feuds with the commissioner.

❖ This Pitcher Was Car-Washed Up

Pitchers Andy Messersmith of the Los Angeles Dodgers and Dave McNally of the Montreal Expos were the key figures in the historic 1975 Seitz decision, which led to the downfall of Major League Baseball's reserve clause and ushered in the current era of free agency.

The reserve clause bound a player to one team for his professional life. Teams would renew contracts for one year for as long as they wanted to retain the player.

In 1975, Messersmith and McNally played without a contract. They argued that their contract could not be renewed if it was never signed. Arbitrator Peter Seitz agreed, and the two were declared free agents. The reserve clause was dead, and free agency followed.

Enter Padres owner Ray Kroc. Kroc was always looking to upgrade his team if the price was right, and he was very interested in talking with Messersmith. The story broke that, in fact, Kroc had offered the pitcher a million-dollar contract.

That night, I went to the ballpark, determined to get an interview with Mr. Kroc, who had not talked publicly about the Messersmith story.

Buzzie Bavasi was Kroc's gatekeeper when the owner was at the ball park. I knew Kroc would be in his suite, and I knew Bavasi would not allow the media to talk with him. I also knew that Kroc often enjoyed several cocktails before and during the game, which meant he would be in a very good mood. The trick was to watch and wait until Bavasi left Kroc's suite, which he usually did as soon as the game got underway. I figured that's when I would make my move.

That evening, I could tell Bavasi was unusually nervous. He normally came through the press box and greeted the media members. But that night he made a pass through the press area without stopping to speak to anyone. The Messersmith story obviously had him on his toes.

At the end of the first inning, Bavasi left the suite and came back through the press area. I had to move now. I told my photographer to follow me. We got on the elevator and rode up to the suite level. I walked to Kroc's suite. The door was open, and he was standing near the bar . . . all alone.

"Mr. Kroc, would you talk with me about the Messersmith story?" I waited for his response as I looked around for Bavasi, who I knew would be coming back soon.

"Hell, yes, I'll talk about it. What do you want to know?"

"Have you offered him a million-dollar contract to play for the Padres?"

"I won't tell you what I offered him, but I will tell you this. If he was in the parking lot right now, begging for a job . . . I wouldn't let Andy Messersmith wash my car. Is that good enough for you? Now why don't you go talk to Ted Turner?"

I had what I wanted, and Bavasi was nowhere in sight. I rushed back to the station, not believing my good fortune, and aired it on the eleven o'clock news. CBS picked up the interview and it became an overnight national story.

A few days later Andy Messersmith signed a three-year, million-dollar contract with the Atlanta Braves. Now for the rest of the story . . . you need to talk to Ted Turner.

Ray Kroc was tireless in his pursuit of excellence. He bought out the McDonald Brothers Corporation in 1954 and built it into the largest chain of successful fast food restaurants in the world.

When he bought the Padres, Kroc expected to one day see his team in the World Series. San Diego faced Detroit in the 1984 series with the Tigers, winning four games to one. Sadly, Ray Kroc never saw it. He had died the previous January.

Early in my tenure in San Diego, I was told by Buzzie Bavasi that Mr. Kroc had mentioned he liked me as a sportscaster, and perhaps for that reason I was invited to Kroc's home in La Jolla on several occasions to conduct interviews.

La Jolla is an affluent seaside resort community nestled along the curving coastline of the Pacific Ocean, within the northern city limits of San Diego. Mr. Kroc's spectacular home sat high on a hillside with a stunning panoramic view of the ocean below. We conducted our interviews on his marble terrace, and the ocean made for a nice backdrop.

I have always been intrigued by all kinds of people from all corners of society. I enjoy studying the habits of high achievers, and I took those occasions to talk with Mr. Kroc about his triumphs and the necessary qualities to be successful in any endeavor.

He enjoyed telling his story. After all, he was living proof that no matter how old you are or what station in life you occupy, you should never stop dreaming and believing.

He started McDonald's when he was fifty-two years old. Before that, he had been a struggling paper cup salesman, real estate broker, piano player, and milkshake mixer salesman.

Mr. Kroc told me that his success—and that of McDonald's—was built around the core principles of quality, service, cleanliness, value, and teamwork. It was teamwork, or the lack thereof, that had made him apologize to Padres fans for the team's inept play that opening day in 1974.

## In Hines' Sight

I admired Ray Kroc tremendously. His business philosophy carried him virtually from the bottom all the way to the top. Plain and simple, he had the mentality of a street fighter who used all those skills to amass one of the greatest fortunes in America in a three-decade period from the fifties through the seventies.

"Luck," he said, "is a dividend of sweat. The more you sweat, the luckier you get."

He made it a weekly, if not daily, habit to walk in unannounced to one of his restaurants to see how it was being run. If he saw an employee just standing around he would say, "If you've got time to lean, you've got time to clean."

Even during our interview sessions at his home, Mr. Kroc's enthusiasm was always evident. If ever there was a man who believed in and demanded total team effort, it was Ray Kroc. I have never forgotten how he said, with passion and conviction, "None of us is as good as all of us."

One final Ray Kroc quote sums up the man better than anything I could ever convey: "It was not her sex appeal but the obvious relish with which she devoured the hamburger that made my pulse begin to hammer with excitement." The man certainly had his priorities in order.

One of my favorite photographs hangs on my office wall at home. It is a picture of me introducing Ray Kroc at a San Diego civic luncheon, with Hollywood actor and producer Danny Thomas looking on.

## ❖ Oh, to Be Able to Soar

You could hardly drive along the Southern California coast without seeing those multicolored specks in the sky. Men and women hanging from a few yards of cloth affixed to a frame of metal tubing out for a gentle ride on nature's toll-free airstreams. They were the free-spirited performers engaging in the sport called hang gliding, which probably comes closest to making man's timeless dream of personal flight a reality.

In the spring of 1976, I went through a hang-gliding school and filmed my efforts for a series on my daily sportscast on KFMB-TV in San Diego. In addition, I wrote an article about my hang-gliding experience that was published in *Aviation Year Book 1978.*

My instructor was an experienced young man by the name of Bill Armstrong. Having taught me the basics, Bill took me to Torrey Pines, a favorite launch site, where I watched gliders leap off the jagged cliffs and fly like birds and wondered if this was something I really wanted to do.

My next lesson took place in Cantamar, Mexico, about forty miles south of Tijuana. It is a beautiful spot. Sand dunes run for miles along the beach, and it's off the dunes that hump upwards of fifty to sixty feet that a beginner learns to fly. The elevation is right; more importantly, the landing is soft.

Bill took me through the checklist as I stood atop the sand dune ready for flight . . . I hoped anyway. I could feel the adrenaline racing through my body. Bill instructed me to run as fast as I could down the dune and to push out on the control bar when I was airborne.

When the wind was just right, Bill said, "Go!" and I began running with all my might. Suddenly, I forgot everything he'd told me. All I could think of was the ground under me and where I would fall. The kite lifted, and I felt as if I was falling backwards. I pulled back on the bar, and the kite stabilized.

For the first time, I realized my feet were not touching the sand. I was flying. My god, what a sensation! It was the most unnatural and yet natural thing I had ever experienced.

I looked down and saw the sand rushing beneath me. I heard cheers and felt a feeling of accomplishment that is hard to describe. Then . . . I crashed into the on-rushing tide.

It certainly wasn't the greatest first flight ever, but there were others to follow, longer lasting and higher. But none will ever compare to your first moment of flight. Sometimes in life you just have to take a leap.

Come to the edge, he said.
They said: We are afraid.
Come to the edge, he said.
They came. He pushed them,
And they flew . . .

—Guillaume Apollinaire, avant garde French poet

### ❖ A Big Surprise for Mama

In April, my parents, Lyman and Floreine, drove to San Diego for a visit. Neither had been farther west than Texas. We did the usual sightseeing things around San Diego, including Point Loma, the San Diego Zoo, Del Coronado Hotel, whale watching, and the highlight of our tour, Black's Beach.

Black's Beach is a secluded portion of beach beneath the bluffs of Torrey Pines on the Pacific Ocean in La Jolla.

We drove to a point overlooking Black's Beach. When we had walked to the edge of the cliff, I handed Mama the binoculars and told her to look at those people lying on blankets below. She eagerly placed the binoculars to her eyes and adjusted the lens. Pat and I watched closely as her mouth dropped open and she exclaimed, "My God, Hope, those people are naked!"

My dad's quick response was, "Gimme those binoculars, Floreine."

Pat and I couldn't contain our laughter any longer. We were howling. Mother looked at me with that disapproving frown I had seen many times growing up, while dad continued to check out the scenery.

Of course, Black's Beach was a well-known Southern California nude beach. For my very southern, prim and proper mother, it was quite an embarrassing shock. But she was a good sport about it. I told her it was payback for sending me to the principal's office that day when she taught me in high school. In the years that followed, we had many laughs over Mama's experience at Black's Beach.

### ❖ Broadcast Dream Job

Remember when I accepted the sports anchor position in San Diego and told station management I also wanted to go after the Chargers radio play-by-play job that was open?

A number of very qualified people, both local and national, applied for the Chargers broadcast job, and in the early months of 1976 I was getting into the mix rather late. However, I had something going for me of which I had no knowledge.

The assistant general manager for the Chargers was Paul "Tank" Younger. Tank had played college football for Eddie

Robinson at Grambling University and was one the first NFL players to come from a predominantly black college. He had played eight years for the Los Angeles Rams and one year in Pittsburgh. Tank was also the first African American to become an NFL front-office administrator.

In my first meeting with Tank Younger, I told him of my friendship with Tennessee State football coach John Merritt. He then told me of his own close ties to Merritt. As much for that reason as for any other, we hit it off. I couldn't wait to phone Merritt and tell him about my conversation with Younger. I told him about the Chargers' radio availability and how much I wanted the job.

"Don't worry. I'll take care of it," Big John responded. "Not only is Tank a close friend, Johnny Sanders [the general manager of the Chargers] is close to me as well. Get ready, baby, you gonna be the Chargers' new play-by-play man."

As it turned out, getting the job wasn't the slam-dunk Big John promised. Still, with his help, along with tapes of the broadcasts I had done for Tennessee State and the fact that I was already anchoring sports for KFMB-TV, the Chargers and the radio station together decided I was the man for the job.

The next step was to pair me with a color commentator. Both Johnny Sanders and Tank Younger wanted former Tulane running back Tommy Mason, the first overall pick in the 1961 NFL draft chosen by the Vikings. Tommy lived in LA and was married to former Olympic gymnast Cathy Rigby.

Tommy and Cathy drove down from Los Angeles one Sunday and we met at my house in Mera Mesa. It didn't take long for us two Southern boys (Tommy was from Lake Charles, Louisiana) to form a bond. We clicked and became the Chargers broadcast team.

❖ An Offer to Return

Several months after I had been named the Chargers play-by-play broadcaster, I got a phone call from Harold Crump, station manager at WLAC-TV in Nashville. Harold wanted to know if I would consider coming back to Channel 5. I had only been gone about six months and was both flattered and surprised by his question. He told me what they wanted to pay me, which was considerably more than I was making when I left. That caused me to wonder why they hadn't made me that same offer before I took the San Diego job. I told Harold I would think about it and get back to him. Pat and I discussed it, and she thought I should really consider the offer. I knew I was in the driver's seat, so I called Harold back and told him it would take a few more thousand than they were offering plus a new car. I got the idea for the new car because the station had given popular weather man Bob Lobertini a car. Harold said he would see what he could do. A few days later he called back saying he would agree to the deal. Now the ball was back in my court.

To be honest, I never seriously considered the offer, because I was not about to walk away from the Chargers play-by-play position, something I had dreamed about for some time. And that's exactly what I told Harold. There would be several additional phone calls from other front office personnel at the station who tried to persuade me to change my mind, but I was solid in my conviction—that door was closed.

The '70s were tough years for the Chargers, and 1976 was no different. Tommy Prothro was head coach. He had been the head coach at both Oregon State and UCLA, and he had also previously coached the L.A. Rams. Upon arrival in San Diego in 1974, he'd promptly hired Bill Walsh as his offensive coordinator. Walsh later won three Super Bowls as head coach of the San Francisco 49ers. Also on Prothro's staff was offensive line coach Howard Mudd and secondary coach Ernie Zampese, both of whom would become highly respected career assistant coaches in the league.

Prothro, a Memphis native, was backfield coach under Red Sanders at Vanderbilt from 1946 to 1948. Interestingly, he was also an expert bridge player, and for several years he partnered with actor Omar Sharif in international competition.

Bill Walsh was an offensive genius and a fascinating coach to watch. I'll never forget observing him during training camp that first year. Not only did he teach his receivers how to run precise pass routes, he would then teach the cornerbacks how to cover those moves. During many of the Chargers' return road trips, I would sit with Walsh on the plane, fascinated at his ability to dissect a game, and it was fun to watch his enthusiasm spark with every question I asked.

During the mid 1970s, the Chargers' offense had three future Hall of Fame inductees: quarterback Dan Fouts, tight end Kellen Winslow, and wide receiver Charlie Joiner. The rest of the lineup wasn't much to speak of.

The Chargers were owned by Eugene V. Klein, a self-made multimillionaire whose business interests were as varied as his sports properties. Gene was the major stockholder of National General Corporation, an insurance and entertainment company based in LA. He also was a founding partner of the Seattle Supersonics of the NBA. Later, Klein was heavily involved in thoroughbred racing. His trainer was D. Wayne Lukas, and his stables at one time numbered 145 horses. In 1988, a filly belonging to Klein, Winning Colors, won the Kentucky Derby.

## ❖ A Riverside Reunion

In June 1976, Nascar made its yearly Winston Cup stop at Riverside International Raceway in Riverside, California. Darrell Waltrip, age twenty-nine, was in his first full race season driving the DiGard Gatorade Chevrolet. I took a station photographer and we drove to Riverside Raceway that week, where I would do a series of interviews with several drivers, including Waltrip.

I caught up with Darrell following his practice session and we greeted each other like long-lost relatives. Just as the camera was about to roll on my first question, DW said, "Wait a minute, Hope. We need to get something straight before we start." I couldn't imagine what he was talking about. "Doing interviews with you back in Nashville, that was one thing. But this Winston Cup deal is big time. I can't afford to cut up with you like we did back home. Besides, these people don't understand that kind of talk, so don't bait me with any of your questions."

"Okay, Darrell, if that's how you feel," I answered. "So, is Riverside where you plan to make a name for yourself on the west coast?" I asked.

Darrell forgot all about not wanting to answer any questions of a controversial nature and answered the same way he always did. He just couldn't help himself. His response was quick, confident, and—yes—cocky.

## ❖ Go Ahead . . . Make my Day

My wife Pat will not be happy that I have included this story about her, but then again she wouldn't be happy if I didn't include it either. So here goes.

The La Costa Resort and Spa, located in Carlsbad, California, in the San Diego area hills was the site of a celebrity tennis tournament. Reading a list of the Hollywood stars that would be in attendance, Pat decided she would accompany me to the world-famous resort. The evening of the tournament, she and I were standing on a balcony that overlooked the tennis courts watching play, when I felt an elbow dig deep into my ribs. She then grabbed my arm and whispered for me to look at who was standing next to her. I took a step back to look past her without being noticed, and looking quite out of character in a warm-up suit was . . . Clint Eastwood. Pat was beside herself, but I have to give her credit, she managed to keep a certain degree of dignified self-control. But she kept punching my side, and I moved to my right to keep from being bruised.

A few minutes later Pat whispered that she was going to the ladies room and left. I didn't notice, but at some point Clint was gone, and Pat had returned.

Not until we were driving home that evening did Pat tell me of her unexpected meeting with Clint Eastwood. She was returning from the ladies room when she came face-to-face with him. There was a moment, she said, when they looked at each other. Clint Eastwood smiled, she smiled back, and he said, "Hello." Pat said she was so flustered that all she could do was smile and keep walking. Ask me how many times I've heard her tell that story over the years, with varying scenarios.

## ❖ A Failed Opportunity

When you are young, at least in my case, ambition lets nothing stand in the way. But, as I eventually discovered, that same zeal can also cloud your judgment. Working in San Diego was a wonderful professional career move, but it caused personal problems I was not equipped to deal with.

In less than two years I had gotten divorced, remarried, and moved to the west coast. After several years in San Diego, with two young children back in Nashville and a transplanted wife and step-son, the issues became problematic. My work was being affected by the burdens, and when I returned from my latest visit to Nashville in the summer of 1977, station management informed me my services were no longer needed. It was both a blessing and a curse. The door was now open for me to return to Nashville, but the fact that I had failed would torment me for years to come.

## In Hines' Sight

For Hope Hines the sportscaster, going to San Diego was a terrific opportunity. For Hope Hines the family man it was not so good. My ambition had taken us to the other side of the country, and heavy sacrifices were made by all. That's the thing about one's ambition: it's not democratic in nature and casualties often result.

Ambition and motivation must have an equal appointment with timing.

Within a family, a team, a group, or any organization, goals and ambitions must be equally desired and shared in order for the outcome to benefit all concerned.

I will always be thankful for my time in San Diego and the life lessons I learned from that experience. By the way, you might be interested in some of the famous KFMB-TV alumni, which include former weather girl Raquel Tejada (later known as Raquel Welch), talk-show host Regis Philbin, TV host Sarah Purcell, CNN and former CBS anchor Paula Zahn . . . and Hope Hines, of course.

The San Diego Chamber of Commerce has little work to do. Who doesn't want to visit and/or live in that beautiful Southern California city? We loved so many things about our time there, including the 72-degree temperatures year round (except for the Santa Ana winds), the beaches, Torrey Pines golf course, the Del Coronado Hotel, whale watching, driving along the California coast to Los Angeles, weekends in Palm

Springs, traveling along the Baha Peninsula, seeing our first bullfight in Tijuana, the San Diego Zoo, and of course showing it all to family and friends who came visiting.

*To decide is to walk facing forward with nary a crick in your neck from looking back at the crossroads.*

BETSY CANAS GARMON

# 5

# U-Haul to Nashville, Racquetball, and Saints

NASHVILLE/NEW ORLEANS • 1977–1978

I TOOK A FEW WEEKS to wallow in self-pity and survey the damage to my career. The radio station that carried the Chargers games wanted me to continue doing their play-by-play, but without the TV job it would not be enough money. Pat and I agreed we should move back to Nashville, regroup, and start over.

I had become friends with a young stock broker in San Diego who was originally from Kentucky, Mike Marnhout. Mike had a client who owned and operated racquetball facilities in Southern California, and they were big money makers. Our idea was to take his concept to Nashville and build a racquetball center where we would make a lot of money.

I rented a U-Haul and loaded up our furniture, and we headed back across the country to Nashville. When Mike arrived with his family, we began looking for investors for our project. Apparently the concept was too foreign, or maybe we didn't do a good enough job of selling the idea; six months later we were still looking for an investor. Mike and I shook hands. He went back to the west coast, and I got a phone call from former Chargers media director Jerry Wynn, who had taken a similar job with the New Orleans Saints.

Jerry was with the Chargers when I did their radio play-by-play, and the Saints were looking for someone to do their pre-season games on WWL-TV in New Orleans. Jerry called to ask if I was interested, and of course I was.

## ❖ The Saints Before the Aints

"Dodgertown" in Vero Beach, Florida, is where the New Orleans Saints held their training camp. I spent a week there before their first preseason game, getting familiar with the players and coaches.

The legendary Hank Stram was the head coach of the Saints. His illustrious career, however, was coming to a close. He had spent fourteen years as head coach of the Dallas Texans/Kansas City Chiefs, highlighted by a victory in Super Bowl IV. He came to the Saints in 1976, and this would be his final year as coach.

I was ushered into Stram's office following practice on my first day in camp. He was sitting behind a very large mahogany desk with a huge mirror hanging behind it. I later learned that Stram was a man who was constantly concerned about his appearance.

Paul Zimmerman, writing for *Sports Illustrated*, wrote this about Stram: "He was a roly-poly guy with a toupee and a stunning wardrobe. Patrolling the sidelines during the Chiefs' 1970 Super Bowl victory over the Vikings, Hank Stram looked like a nightclub entertainer, snapping off his one-liners."

Stram was considered a motivational master, but his genius produced only seven wins in his two years with the Archie Manning–led Saints. Also on those mid-'70s teams were defensive end Elois Grooms of Tennessee Tech, defensive back Jim Marsalis of Tennessee State, and quarterback Bobby Scott of Tennessee.

Perhaps the most interesting and entertaining feature of the Saints during those years was the team's owner, John Mecom Jr., who founded the team in 1968 at age twenty-six. Mecom paid 7.5 million dollars for the franchise, selling it to Tom Benson for 70 million in 1985.

Mecom was a handsome, dashing riverboat gambler, as high-profile as they come. The *Houston Chronicle* reported that his interests were in oil, gas, race cars, hotels, exotic game, planes, ranches, horses, and, of course, his beloved Saints.

Mecom could often be found in the Saints locker room working out with the players. When the movie *The Pro* (about an aging quarterback), starring Charlton Heston, was filmed in New Orleans, Mecom actually played the role of the third-string quarterback in the film.

One of the perks of doing the Saints TV games and traveling to New Orleans each week was staying in the world-famous Le Pavilion Hotel, which John Mecom Jr. owned. The "Belle of New Orleans," as the hotel is called, sits adjacent to the historic French Quarter. This five-star hotel features crystal chandeliers from Czechoslovakia and marble floors from many locations throughout Europe. Fine art and antiques from around the world add to the décor and elegance of the hotel. One of its trademarks is the extremely rare three-arch Brunswick Bar, circa 1880. It was salvaged from a Chicago hotel frequented by gangster Al Capone. Looking closely, you can see where repairs were made to it after a failed mob hit. The bar was a favorite hangout for politicians and entertainers.

With the racquetball venture down for the count and the Saints preseason coming to a close, it was time to get busy figuring out my next move.

## In Hines' Sight

I was thirty-five years old, and my career had suffered a major setback. I found myself at a crossroads, looking into the future with fearful suspicion.

Crossroads, by their very nature, yield little if any insight into which way you should turn next. The best you can hope for at any crossroad is to look behind where you have been to see if it offers any clues as to whether you should turn left, right, or plunge straight ahead.

My crossroad decision became more difficult as I peered into the unknown. The last thing I needed to do at that juncture was make another bad choice. Panic often obstructs one's reasoning, leading to snap judgments. Patience is the preferred choice. Patience and composure allow us to endure a little longer during difficult circumstances, allowing us to become equipped to arrive at the best possible conclusion.

# Family Business

I MADE A QUICK DECISION about my future. It came after several phone conversations with my family in Georgia. My father and two younger brothers were involved in various forms of real estate. We discussed my moving to Valdosta and joining the family business.

Real estate intrigued me, and I thought at the time it would be a good move to learn about a business so many had made lots of money in while trying to decide if television was still my future.

So it was decided that Pat and I would join my family in a business venture, building homes on land my father had purchased. I would be learning real estate from the ground up.

It occurred to me early in the move to Valdosta that I might want to keep my hand in television just in case this real estate thing didn't work out. I picked up the phone one day and called the news director at the CBS affiliate in Tallahassee, WCTV-TV. I told him of my background in TV sports anchoring, and he asked me to send him a videotape of my work.

He called several days later saying he didn't have an opening in the sports department, but he asked if I would be interested in anchoring the weekend news. I said I would be, and two weeks later I began anchoring the weekend news in Tallahassee.

I was building houses Monday through Friday—with a shovel in my hands, digging foundations. I learned about building codes, buying lumber and other materials, and every aspect of home-building, such as septic tank regulations, electrical and plumbing specifications, and landscaping.

Sound like a lot of fun? Well, not to me, actually. But I was learning, and I figured how else would I master the building business?

Saturdays and Sundays, I drove to Tallahassee and anchored the news, where I was back in my element.

One of the most talented guys I ever worked with was Gene Deckerhoff, who anchored the weekend sports in Tallahassee. Gene was destined for much greater things, however. Several years later, he became the radio play-by-play voice of the Florida State Seminoles and the Tampa Bay Bucs of the NFL . . . juggling both jobs at the same time. In 2000, Gene was inducted into the Florida Sports Hall of Fame, becoming just the fourth sports broadcaster to be enshrined in the FSHOF.

Anchoring the weekend weather during my stint in Tallahassee was Davis Nolan. In the early '80s, Davis moved to Nashville, becoming a favorite personality with WKRN-TV.

It was during my association with WCTV-TV that I first met Florida State head football coach Bobby Bowden, who had taken over the program in 1976. Bowden's TV show was produced at the station, and on many occasions his wife, Ann, accompanied him for the taping. If ever a marriage was made in heaven it was Bobby and Ann's.

❖ A Tallahassee Tragedy

Super Bowl XII was played in the Superdome in New Orleans on Sunday January 15, 1978, between the Dallas Cowboys and the Denver Broncos. It was the first Super Bowl played inside a domed stadium.

That same day, citizens of Tallahassee awoke to the horrifying news that at approximately 3:00 a.m., serial killer Ted Bundy had entered FSU's Chi Omega sorority house. In the next fifteen minutes, he bludgeoned Margaret Bowmann, twenty-one, with a piece of oak firewood as she was sleeping, then strangled her with a nylon stocking. Bundy then beat twenty-year-old Lisa Levy unconscious, strangling her and sexually assaulting her with a hair mist bottle. In an adjoining room, he attacked Kathy Kleiner, who suffered a broken jaw, and Karen Chandler, who suffered a concussion, broken jaw, loss of teeth, and a crushed finger.

When I arrived at the TV station that afternoon, the newsroom, as you can imagine, was in chaos, with reporters and photographers scrambling for information. CBS carried the Super Bowl that year, and it was the first time the game was shown in prime time, which meant that most of our stories about the Chi Omega killings would not be seen until after the game. It was one of the most intense days I have ever spent in a newsroom, as we wrote, rewrote, edited, and re-edited stories as new information was gathered hour by hour. It was quite an experience for a guy who had spent the first part of his TV career reporting on games and showing game highlights. This was the serious side of television news, and I was in on one of the biggest national stories of the year.

### ❖ A Major Flip-Flop

I continued building houses and anchoring news on the weekends, but the economy was suffering. Inflation was 12.4 percent. Interest rates ballooned to almost 12 percent. The U.S. dollar plunged to record lows, and gasoline prices were sky-high. Land prices and home building were caught in an economic squeeze play.

It was time to get back on that TV horse and ride again full time. I began sending out résumé tapes to stations across the country. Since I had been anchoring news, I applied for news anchor jobs just to see what response I would get. I also sent tapes for a couple of sports openings as well. The ABC affiliate in Pensacola, Florida, called and flew me down for a visit. They offered me the lead (news) anchor position Monday through Friday. I accepted and was scheduled to start in three weeks.

Three days later, however, I got a call from Dave Blackshear, whom I had worked with at WGAU radio in Athens and gone to school with at the University of Georgia. Dave was the news director at WRET-TV in Charlotte, the Ted Turner–owned station.

Dave had heard I was trying to get back into TV full time and called to say he had an opening for a sports director. He asked if I would be interested. I told him I had just agreed to anchor the news in Pensacola. We continued to talk, and he asked how solid was my agreement with the station; I told him I hadn't yet signed a contract.

He said he wanted to send me a plane ticket to Charlotte for a visit before I signed with Pensacola. I agreed and flew to Charlotte for a meeting. Before I left I called the station in Pensacola and told them I was extremely sorry, but I had changed my mind. I told them that in my heart I was still a sports guy and truly felt that was my calling. They were disappointed but they understood. No damage done.

---

## In Hines' Sight

It was a gut feeling, and I knew it was the right decision to make. Still, I have often wondered how my career and my life would have been different if I had chosen to anchor news over sports. It never occurred to me until this writing how blessed and fortunate I was to have two job offers at the same time.

Even more extraordinary, how many times in a television career has someone been offered an anchoring position in news and sports at the same time?

What I learned from that unique career option was something as profound as it was simplistic: be true to yourself.

When you narrow a decision after considering all the information available to you, in the end, it is that gut feeling that speaks the loudest. It takes tremendous courage to be true to yourself. Always follow that awareness. It will guide you in the direction you are intended to go, and the joyous benefit is a certain freedom you will always experience when you trust yourself.

# Humpy, Dale, and Dean

Dave Blackshear asked me to commit to two years with WRET in Charlotte. I told him I would, but I didn't want to sign a contract. As it turned out, I would break my agreement long before the two years were up.

When I arrived in Charlotte, I learned very quickly that there were only two things sports fans cared about there: racing and college basketball, not necessarily in that order.

H. A. "Humpy" Wheeler cast a giant shadow across the Nascar landscape in Charlotte. Humpy was president and general manager of Charlotte Motor Speedway, later Lowe's Motor Speedway. Humpy was to racing what Don King was to boxing . . . without the electric hair. He was the first to have pre-race shows and world-record car jumps.

Humpy began his promotional career selling tickets for a bicycle race at age nine. He became so respected in auto racing that he eventually landed in ten halls of fame, including the prestigious International Motorsports and American Racing Hall of Fame. Talking with Humpy was always a treat. His interviews were colorful, and you felt like you had just talked to the most knowledgeable man in the sport.

I first met Humpy shortly after going on the air at WRET. I had gone to the speedway to do an interview about the upcoming World 600 in May, and we ended up talking about the driver who was about to change the face of Nascar, Dale Earnhardt.

Humpy said he had never seen a youngster so determined, so hungry, not just to drive but to win. Later that season, Earnhardt won Rookie of the Year. He followed that by winning his first Winston Cup Championship in 1980, and he remains the only driver in history to follow a Rookie of the Year title with a Nascar championship.

One of the highlights of my career was my first meeting with Earnhardt. The first thing I noticed was that half-crooked smirk of a smile. He was a man of few words who spoke in short, clipped sentences. Cock-sure of himself, he had that immediate look of a winner. By the time our interview was over that day and my photographer had gotten enough shots of Earnhardt's #2 blue and yellow Chevrolet Monte Carlo, we had developed a good rapport. I asked tough and direct questions, and Earnhardt respected that approach. I recall asking several leading but playful questions and getting high-spirited answers in response. It was part of Earnhardt's interview style that would be his modus operandi for the remainder of his career.

The photo is priceless. Maybe you've seen it. The one taken in 1979 that shows a young Dale Earnhardt Sr. peeling back the top of his fire-suit and revealing a T-shirt that says:

Damn
I'm
Good

He certainly was. I always delighted in the special relationship Dale and I seemed to share. Every time I have ever been around him, whether in the garage at various tracks around the country, at a charity event, or at a TV studio where we were conducting an interview, he always had that distinguished presence all the great ones have. It is a certain undeniable look that says . . . champion.

"His tenacity was unmatched. It had to be. How else would a ninth-grade dropout from Kannapolis, NC, build a multimillion-dollar business?" wrote Marty Smith for *Turner Sports Interactive*.

## ❖ Sent Packing by the Dean

Now, speaking of that *other* most popular sport in Charlotte . . . basketball. Fans of the Atlantic Coast Conference held the belief that their basketball coaches were just as important as football coaches in the Southeastern Conference. When I talked with the University of North Carolina sports information director about conducting an on-campus interview with Tarheel coach Dean Smith, I didn't realize the ground rules would be so meticulous.

I was told exactly what time to arrive at his office, which was one hour before the scheduled interview. I was then informed that I would have that time to set up my equipment in the designated interview room and I would be advised of the exact time coach Smith would sit down for his ten-minute interview. I was then reminded to be ready to start the moment he walked into the room. There would be no allowances otherwise.

If ever there was a coach who choreographed his way through life it was Dean Smith. Everything, both on the basketball court and off, was calibrated to the minute, and that included my interview with one of college basketball's greatest coaches.

I had never met coach Smith before that day, and when he entered the interview room he was dressed for practice; it seemed his mind was already engaged around the afternoon workout. He was cordial yet businesslike. I sensed he wanted to get this interview over with as quickly as possible. Remember, I had ten minutes . . . max.

I began the interview with the usual softball questions about the season and somehow drifted into a question about his coaching demeanor when his team played a game on national television. His answer was, "What are you talking about? I don't coach any differently whether we're on TV or not." He was not pleased with the question. I tried again.

"Coach Smith, you never become animated and play to the camera when you know it's on you, say during a crucial timeout."

"Who do you think you are, Tom Snyder? [At the time Tom Snyder was the late night talk show host of NBC's *Tomorrow* show.] I just gave you my answer to that question." It was at that moment he removed the clip-on microphone, stood up, said, "This interview is over," and walked out of the room.

Needless to say, I did not endear myself to Carolina basketball fans when I aired the entire two-minute interview with Dean Smith that evening on the six o'clock sportscast.

But you need to know the rest of my Dean Smith story. The following week the ACC basketball tournament was held at the Greensboro Coliseum in Greensboro, NC, and I covered the game for the station. For me to get to my seat in the press section I had to walk behind the Carolina bench. The Tarheels were on the floor for their pregame warm-up. As I walked by, Coach Smith was sitting in his chair on the floor watching his team, and he must have seen my approach out of the corner of his eye. When I was almost even with him, he suddenly stood, held out his hand, and said, "Nice to see you," and sat back down.

I wouldn't have been any more shocked if he had pulled out a gun. I was totally stunned, and I have no idea what I said in reply, but what a classy thing for him to do. I never did another sit-down interview with Dean Smith, but the two minutes I spent with him that week before, and his gesture toward me that night before the game, will always be Hall of Fame moments in my life.

## In Hines' Sight

Humpy, Dale, and Dean—all three approved by the experts as the best at what they did. Humpy was a true visionary in stock car racing, the perfect example of a man who could think outside the boundaries of the ordinary. The beginning rise of Nascar's popularity can be directly traced to the promotional imagination of Humpy Wheeler, and for a time I was privileged to have a front row seat to his genius.

You could say Dale Earnhardt was a man's man. You could also say he was a woman's man. Men wanted to be like him. Women wanted to be with him. There was definitely enough to like (or hate) about Dale Earnhardt for everybody. Like other athletic giants such as Muhammad Ali, Mickey Mantle, Michael Jordan, and Jack Nicklaus, Earnhardt set the standard in his sport by which others would measure and be measured. You see someone like the "Intimidator" once in a lifetime, if you're lucky. For many he was the American dream, and more. He was their hero.

When Dean Smith waved his hand, players orchestrated their movements to his command using art and skills they had been taught by the maestro. For thirty-six years as head coach at North Carolina, Smith ran a clean program, graduating 97 percent of his players and winning 77 percent of his games. His record alone is good enough to place him in the legend category. But what is not as well-publicized is the enormous heart he has for all who played and coached for him. They are his pride and joy.

Head coach at Carolina Roy Williams, who played under Smith, says that he cared more about teaching life lessons to his players than winning either of his two National Championships. Most who know him use one word to describe Dean Smith: *class*. Hear, hear.

## ❖ Moving On

I had been in Charlotte one year when I received a phone call from Jack Dawson of WMAR-TV, the NBC affiliate in Baltimore. He said they were looking for someone to coproduce and host a weekly Sunday night half-hour sports magazine show. He had seen my work on videotape and wanted to know if I would be interested in the job. Of course I was. It was Baltimore, home of the Colts and Orioles—who wouldn't be?

I flew to Baltimore and interviewed for the job. Several days later, Jack called and made me an offer. I accepted. Now came the tough part. I had to tell Dave Blackshear I was leaving. Remember, I had promised I would stay with WRET for two years. When I informed him I had taken a job in Baltimore, he was extremely disappointed, but in the end he understood. He just didn't think I would leave so soon. Neither did I.

Charlotte was an outstanding place to live and work. We lived in a wonderful two-story home on fifty acres in Matthews, North Carolina, just down the road from Charlotte. Farmland rolled out in all directions. There were cows in the pasture and a dune buggy to ride on the weekends. Day and night, the fresh air was invigorating, and cutting down that Christmas tree in December made it our best ever.

*Do not plant your dreams in the field of indecision, where nothing ever grows but the weeds of "what-if."*

DODINSKY

# A Baltimore Blast

## BALTIMORE 1980–1983

THE CONCEPT OF A LOCAL half-hour Sunday night sports show, now fairly common, had never been done in Baltimore, or anywhere else I had ever heard of at that time. When I arrived in the summer of 1980, baseball fever was running hot. The Orioles were involved in a heated battle with the Yankees for the American League East lead.

We were planning our first *Sunday Sports-Scene Magazine* show and decided a sit-down interview with the Orioles highly popular and legendary manager Earl Weaver (Hall of Fame, 1996) would be the centerpiece for our first show. Of course, I knew of his reputation as one of the most colorful managers ever in the big leagues. He was adored by Oriole fans, as much for his on-field antics as for his shrewd managerial ability. He had called the shots that took the Orioles to four World Series, winning it all in 1970.

When Earl stormed out of the dugout headed for a conversation (if you could call it that) with the man in blue, the fans went wild. He loved to kick dirt on umpires, and he would turn his cap around backward to get as close to them as possible without touching. Weaver was ejected from ninety-one regular season games and several more during post-season play. When all five feet six inches of Earl Weaver tangled with an umpire, he was always looking up. It was quite a show.

I was set to interview Weaver in his office at Memorial Stadium several hours before an afternoon game. I had met him briefly before and had been informed about his customary "grumpy" disposition toward members of the media. Naturally, I was somewhat anxious about my sit-down with not only one of the best managers ever in baseball, but one with an attitude.

Our interview began with me asking him about the hot midsummer race with the Yankees. He then discussed his starting pitching rotation, which consisted of Jim Palmer, Mike Flanagan, Dennis Martinez, Scotty McGregor, and Steve Stone. He talked about the need for the Orioles to continue to hit and be consistent with the bats, and to not fall into a prolonged slump.

Back in April, MLB players had gone on an eight-day strike during spring training over free-agency compensation. I asked Earl for his stance on the brief walkout, but he refused to answer the question, saying something about how his attention was now on a tight division race and he couldn't care less about what had happened in April.

I had been warned, and now I understood what they meant about his prickly temperament. So I tried to ask the question another way. I said something like, "But, Coach, don't you think the players—" I never finished my question because he jumped to the edge of his chair, red in the face, then pointed his finger at me and blurted, "What did you call me? *Coach?* I ain't no coach. I'm the manager of the Baltimore Orioles, and if you're gonna work in this town, you better understand that." He was right. The second I called him Coach I knew I'd screwed up. I was so accustomed to calling everybody Coach it just slipped out. I apologized, and we continued with the interview. And so went my introduction to the "Earl of Baltimore."

### ❖ Tomato Wars

My relationship with Weaver after that first interview grew into one of mutual respect over the next few years. I really liked Earl. He was fun to interview . . . as long as the Os were winning. His comments were filled with colorful adjectives. When things were not going so well, he was a challenge to engage in conversation. No mater what, interviewing Earl Weaver was never dull.

Every year at Baltimore's old Memorial Stadium, no matter what the Orioles were doing on the field, there was a major story taking place in a fenced-off area in left-field foul territory. Players and fans alike kept up with the great "tomato war" that was waged each season between Earl Weaver and head groundskeeper Pat Santarone. The competition between them was legendary and as well-documented as any umpire feud Weaver ever had.

Santarone first began growing tomatoes at Memorial Stadium in 1970, the year the Orioles won the World Series.

Weaver had his tomato garden at his home in Perry Hall.

"Players loved to monitor the competition between Santarone and Weaver over the tomatoes they planted down the left-field line." Former catcher Rick Dempsey told the *Baltimore Sun*, "They argued like brothers over those tomatoes."

In a 1979 interview with the *Sun*, Santarone said he taught Weaver, who didn't know a rake from a lawnmower, how to garden. "But I didn't teach him all my secrets," Santarone said. "That's what makes him so grouchy, sitting up all night trying to figure out what I haven't told him yet."

Santarone was also a consultant to the Pimlico Race Track in Baltimore, and in that same interview he bragged that his tomatoes had been fertilized with manure from Spectacular Bid and Secretariat. "From the looks of Weaver's tomatoes, he's getting his manure from a horse that ran ninth in a nine-horse race."

In 1981, I wanted to do an entire half-hour *Sunday Sports-Scene Magazine* show with Weaver at his home. We talked about it, he agreed, and we picked an off-day for the Orioles to do the interview.

Several rooms in Weaver's home were filled with memorabilia from his distinguished career. We talked about the Orioles World Series appearances and the 1970 championship. We discussed current and former players, the state of the game, and finally his devoted hobby of gardening. It was early summer, and he invited me on a tour of his half-acre garden, which had many varieties of vegetables growing in addition to his prized tomatoes. As he talked about each vegetable and its proper care, it was clear that he had become quite the expert. Another thing that was clear to anyone watching was that he enjoyed that part of the interview much more than talking baseball. The show was a hit with viewers and was one of the best pieces I had ever done.

Earl was certainly difficult to deal with on occasion, but that day he demonstrated his softer side when he gave me an autographed bat.

There are so many well-known Earl Weaver stories. One of my favorites was the day Weaver told outfielder Pat Kelly that Kelly didn't have time to attend a chapel service because batting practice started in fifteen minutes. Kelly asked Weaver if he didn't want him to walk with the Lord, and Weaver said, "I'd rather you walk with the bases loaded."

## ❖ Stone Cold Steve

There were some interesting personalities on those Oriole teams in the early 1980s, and some future Hall of Famers. In 1980, Steve Stone won twenty-five and lost seven, winning the American League Cy Young award and the *Sporting News* pitcher of the year.

Steve was a good-looking guy who was articulate and well-liked by the media, but he was not your typical pro athlete. Steve was the Orioles' foodie and restaurateur. He was a published poet, a chess player, and one of the best table-tennis players around. He was also considered a little goofy by some because of his perceived eccentric ways. Steve practiced "visualization" before every game he pitched, and many snickered at his "metaphysical" approach to the art of pitching.

Visualization, as the name implies, is a mental exercise in which subjects make every effort to "see" a goal come true in their mind's eye. For example, a pitcher might visualize himself having a perfect game. Studies have shown that the mind cannot tell the difference between practice that is actually performed and practice that is imagined.

Steve was not at all bashful in boasting about his pregame ritual, and I decided it would make a good Sunday night segment for our show during Steve's 1980 Cy Young season. I approached Steve with the idea, and he eagerly agreed to do the story.

On the days Steve pitched home games, he would travel the exact same route to the ballpark, stopping by the same McDonald's on his way to purchase the same sandwich and milkshake. Our plan was to follow Steve and record his game-day ritual. I drove the car while my photographer shot footage of his journey.

We arrived at McDonald's and followed Steve inside. We recorded Steve ordering and being served. As we were leaving, the store manager came charging out from behind the counter, in a high state of agitation. He demanded we give him the video from the camera, because we had not gotten permission to shoot inside the restaurant. I later learned that TV stations must always get permission to shoot anything inside or outside a business establishment. (What did I know? I was a sports guy, for goodness sakes.)

I was stunned by the confrontation and tried to explain what we were doing with the Orioles' star pitcher, but none of that seemed to matter. The manager was adamant that I should give him the video, and I was just as determined not to give it up. This was not how I envisioned the story developing.

Steve was already outside getting in his car when we came out, with the manager right on our heels, threatening to sue us. I told him to do what he had to do but I was not giving up the video, and we left.

Steve lost the game that day, and later he jokingly said it would be best if he never did another interview with me.

Steve threw a heavy dose of curve balls during his 1980 Cy Young award season. In 1981, his struggle with tendonitis indicated that his days on the mound were drawing to a close. In 1983, Stone became a color commentator for WGN, broadcasting the Chicago Cubs for the next fourteen years with Hall of Famer Harry Caray.

> Pitching is really just an internal struggle between pitcher
> and his stuff. If my curve ball is breaking and I'm throwing
> it where I want, the batter is irrelevant.
>
> —Steve Stone

## ❖ Cal & Cal

During my time in Baltimore, I had the privilege of covering some unique personalities and athletes, including Cal and Cal: the Ripkens, Jr. and Sr.

Cal Sr. spent thirty-six years in the Orioles organization, from a minor league catcher, to third-base coach, to manager. My good friend, the late John Steadman, a longtime sports columnist for the *Baltimore Sun*, called Ripken "the toughest of old Orioles" and added, "He was a throwback to another era."

Cal Sr. was tough and blunt, with a quick temper. As Frank Litsky of the *New York Times* described him, "He was given to salty language." He chain-smoked and had a voice that, one observer wrote, "sounded like the bucket of a backhoe scraping a boulder."

Whenever I needed an interview to probe the slump a particular player was having, Cal was my man. He never gave the standard company answer to anything. Ask a direct question from Cal, and you got a direct answer, salty language and all.

Cal Sr. followed Earl Weaver as manager of the Orioles in 1987, and what a thrill it had to be that year when Cal became the first father to manage two sons simultaneously in the majors, as Billy Ripken became Cal Jr.'s double-play partner. But in typical Cal Sr. fashion, he quipped: "We just happen to be in the same business at the same place. Maybe years from now, I'll smile about all this. But for now they're just a second baseman and a shortstop on this ball club."

Cal Jr. came up to the Orioles in 1981 from the Triple-A Rochester Red Wings. That year turned out to be a strike year, in which 713 games were cancelled in the middle of the regular season. Watching Cal around the infield, and with a bat, you knew he was a special player with an unlimited future, which baseball history has already recorded; he was a nineteen-time Major League All-Star who broke Lou Gehrig's fifty-six-year-old consecutive game streak record, playing in his 2,131st game on September 6, 1995.

His personality was the direct opposite of his father's. Cal Jr. was always polite and cordial and a pleasure to interview. He always had time for small talk before and after an interview.

Did you know Cal Jr. arrived in Baltimore as a third baseman? All of a sudden one day before a game, "I thought Earl made a lineup mistake, writing '6' (shortstop) instead of '5' (third base)," Ripken told Doug Brown of the *Baltimore Sun*. "He hadn't prepared me for the move."

When Cal approached his father about the switch, Cal Sr. said, "Don't worry, just catch the ball and throw it to first."

A note about my late friend John Steadman, columnist for the *Baltimore Sun*. I met John when I first arrived in Baltimore, and when he found out I had worked in Nashville there was an immediate connection. John was very helpful in providing me with the history and understanding of the Baltimore sports landscape. John was a huge country music fan, and over the years had developed a friendship with Eddie Arnold and Bill Anderson. One day, John called and invited me to accompany him to a Bill Anderson concert. Bill had made arrangements to meet us on his bus before the performance, and it turned out to be a reunion of three guys who loved country music but spent the time talking sports.

John attended every Baltimore Colts and Ravens football game from 1947 to 2001 (he died January 1, 2001), a streak of 719 games. He was also one of only eight writers to attend every Super Bowl game, up through XXXIV (thirty-four). John also served a decade as color commentator on Colts radio broadcasts from the mid '50s to the mid '60s, with play-by-play man Chuck Thompson. He was honored by the Associated Press sports editors as the posthumous recipient of the Red Smith award, America's most prestigious sports writing honor, in June of 2001.

## ❖ Brooksie

One of the most enjoyable aspects of the baseball season every year in Baltimore was working with former Oriole Hall of Fame third baseman Brooks Robinson. Brooks and I shared the same microphone for our live shots from Memorial Stadium for WMAR-TV during the year. I can honestly say I never met a classier individual; he commanded instant respect from everyone he met. How good was Brooksie as a player? Sixteen consecutive Gold Glove Awards. Named to fifteen consecutive All-Star teams. His performance against the Cincinnati Reds won him the 1970 World Series MVP award. He played his entire twenty-three-year career for the Orioles and is generally acclaimed as the greatest defensive third baseman in Major League history.

On October 22, 2011, a statue was unveiled on Washington Boulevard in downtown Baltimore depicting Robinson preparing to throw out a runner at first base.

I learned more about being a Major League ball player from

Brooks than from all the others combined. I'll never forget asking him one day following our live shot why he left the ballpark and seldom stayed to watch a game. Brooks gently placed his hand on my shoulder, as if he was about to give me some fatherly advice. He looked me in the eye and said with a half-smirk, "Hope, I've spent most of my life in somebody's ballpark. It's time to go home."

Over the course of his spectacular career, players and writers alike wrote and spoke about the great Brooks Robinson:

> Brooks Robinson never asked anyone to name a candy bar after him. In Baltimore, people named their children after him.
>
> —Gordon Beard, Associated Press sportswriter

> He can throw his glove out there and it will start ten double plays by itself.
>
> —Sparky Anderson, Cincinnati Reds manager

> He's not at his locker yet, but four guys are over there interviewing his glove.
>
> —Rex Barney, Orioles PA announcer

And this one said it best:

> How many interviews, how many questions—how many times you approached him and got only courtesy and decency in return. A true gentleman who never took himself seriously. I always had the idea he didn't know he was Brooks Robinson.
>
> —Joe Falls, *Detroit News*

## In Hines' Sight

Cal Ripken Jr., Brooks Robinson, Frank Robinson, Eddie Murray, Jim Palmer, and Earl Weaver—all members of the baseball Hall of Fame. How fortunate I was to have spent time in the clubhouse and dugout with all six.

Each had something valuable to teach, and I had lots to learn. I saw how Cal Jr. not only seized an opportunity when presented, but without hesitation gave it absolutely all he had, and when he was out of bullets he found some more. He embraced the circumstances of the moment with more focus and determination than anyone I've ever seen.

Working with and observing how Brooks Robinson easily moved among people I learned about genuine humility. I also came to understand that without the pure passion he had for the game he would have never seen Cooperstown.

Frank Robinson was the hitting coach for the Orioles in 1980. The much-respected Robinson became the first African American manager in the big leagues in 1975 with the Cleveland Indians. Frank took tremendous pride in his job and his place in baseball history. He preached to be prepared, not make excuses, and work hard. He insisted his players think about the game of baseball and how special it is, and how privileged they were to play it. In other words, be thankful for what you have.

In 1979, Eddie Murray refused to speak to the press following an article by a New York columnist, who wrote a story about Murray's family during the World Series with the Pittsburgh Pirates. Eddie was so upset by the piece that he all but quit doing interviews, even with the Baltimore media. Eddie's quiet leadership on the field was respected by all who played with him—and against him.

Jim Palmer was as smooth on the mound as any high-kicking right hander who ever threw a fast ball. What impressed me most about "Cakes" (he got his nickname because of his love for pancakes) was his confidence and poise under pressure. The single Palmer, by the way, was just as smooth off the mound with the ladies. You might be interested to know that Jim, born in New York, was adopted. When his adoptive father died, the nine-year-old Jim, his mother, and sister moved to California. His mother married actor Max Palmer, from whom Palmer took his last name.

I learned an important lesson from Earl Weaver: never to call him "Coach." (Remember the story of our first interview?)

Actually, what I really learned from Earl was to be prepared before an interview. If you didn't ask intelligent, well thought out questions and make sure that you knew everything factual about the situation, Earl would make you look silly, which is every reporter's fear. Be informed and you'll live to interview Earl another day.

### ❖ The Golden Arm

It was a Baltimore landmark that paid tribute to a Baltimore legend: The Golden Arm bar and restaurant in Rodgers Forge, owned by Baltimore's fabulous Golden Arm, former Colts quarterback Johnny Unitas. The place was only a hundred yards or so away from my office at WMAR-TV, the signature establishment in York Road Plaza. It is not recommended to locate a news organization so close to a popular watering-hole . . . we certainly had our share of happy hours there.

At Johnny's bar, many conversations of candor and comedy were held beneath the painted mural that depicted Unitas in a scene from the NFL Championship sudden-death victory of the Colts over the New York Giants in 1958—known as the greatest game ever played.

It was always a treat to watch "the man" show up and mingle among the patrons, shaking hands and signing autographs. He would make his way to the bar, speaking to everyone and calling most by their first name. Although it was an upscale restaurant, The Golden Arm had the feel of a Baltimore neighborhood bar.

I was fortunate enough to work with Unitas for several years doing the Colts preseason telecasts on WMAR. He was a wonderful human being who loved to laugh and did it easily. Unitas loved to tell stories, and he had a million about his playing days.

Ernie Accorsi was the Colts General Manager in the early '80s. Ernie was later the GM for the Cleveland Browns and New York Giants. He was also a good friend of Unitas. Ernie loved to tell this story, which captures a piece of the Johnny Unitas legend.

It was Don Shula's second year as head coach of the Colts. Shula sent receiver Alex Hawkins into a game with a play to give to Unitas. When Hawkins got to the huddle, Unitas shot him an ice-cold stare, demanding to know why he was there. Hawkins said he brought in a play from Shula. Unitas stepped out of the huddle, called for a timeout, and headed for the sideline. Unitas stopped two feet in front of Shula and said, "If you want to run that play . . . you go in and run it." Shula backed down, and from that day on Unitas called the plays.

Johnny was great to travel with. It was always amazing the number of people who came up to him and just wanted to shake his hand. Getting an autograph was a bonus. He had a certain charismatic quality and was always gracious with his admirers. Wherever we went he was recognized, and by then he had changed his hairstyle from his signature flat-top to a much longer comb-over style. His new look was a far cry from the original Johnny U.

In the broadcast booth, Unitas acquired a reputation, just as he had done on the playing field, for honesty and frankness. Whenever I was covering a story I thought Johnny could enhance, I would call him, and he never refused, giving his blunt opinion, which always added spice to the story.

## ❖ The Curse of Irsay

The early and mid 1980s were trying times for Colts fans. Fans paid good money to witness bad football Sunday after Sunday. The team won just sixteen games from 1980 through 1983, and much of the fans' rage was directed toward absentee owner Bob Irsay.

Irsay was known for bad trades, locker-room tantrums, and eventually for being one of the biggest traitors in the history of professional sports. He never knew any of the assistant coaches' names—when he did speak to one, he simply called him Tiger.

When asked to describe Irsay, former Colts quarterback Bert Jones told the *Baltimore Sun*, "He lied and he cheated and he was rude and he was crude . . . and he was Bob Irsay. He doesn't have any morals. It's a sad state for the NFL to be associated with him."

One of the weirdest stories I ever covered happened on November 15, 1981, in a Colts 38–13 loss to the Eagles in Philadelphia. Mike McCormack was head coach. In the second half, an irate Bob Irsay found his way to the coaches' box and began calling plays. After the game, an embarrassed McCormack had to face the media. He tried to downplay Irsay's actions, but it was clearly a horrible black mark against the organization and a low point in NFL history.

During the summer of 1980, the Colts held their annual alumni golf tournament. Not only was I invited to play, I was paired with none other than Bob Irsay. In fact, the week before the tournament I had been told by Ernie Accorsi that they wanted me to play with Bob. Of course I agreed, figuring this could be very interesting.

The word I would use to describe four hours with Bob Irsay is *fascinating*. This complex and conflicted man couldn't have been nicer and more cordial. He was an awful golfer, and I wasn't much better, so we got along wonderfully. He was funny, engaging, and uncharacteristically polite. I also spent some time that day with Bob's wife, Harriet, a lovely lady who possessed all the class in the family.

It was not uncommon for Irsay to fly in with several of his Chicago cronies to watch the team practice during training camp . . . and, yes, take part in workouts. I recall one day when the kickoff team lined up with an extra person . . . wearing a tie with his pants rolled up to his ankles. The whistle blew, the ball was kicked, and a mighty yell was heard from the 12th guy as they flew downfield. When the play ended, he was lying flat on his back, screaming, "More Jack. I gotta have more Jack Daniels! The pain's killing me."

During those years, Bob's son, current Indianapolis Colts owner Jim Irsay, attended Southern Methodist University. During the summer he could be found in the Colts weight room. Jim was a workout fanatic who had bulked up to 295 pounds squatting 750 pounds in power-lifting tournaments.

### ❖ A Call from the Dentist

In the spring of 1980, I got a call from Jerry Argovitz, the agent for running back Curtis Dickey from Texas A&M, who was the Colts number one draft choice, fifth overall. Jerry, a former dentist, and the Colts were getting nowhere in their negotiations. Argovitz had a reputation as outrageous but very good copy, and he knew how to manipulate the media to his advantage.

Argovitz had done his research and knew that I hosted a half-hour magazine show on Sunday nights. His proposition was that I would fly to Houston to meet him, then we would fly in his helicopter to Bryan, Texas, where Dickey lived. Argovitz wanted Baltimore fans to see Dickey's dirt-poor home and lifestyle in the impoverished section of Bryan.

One week later, I flew to Houston to do the story on Curtis Dickey. But when I arrived, Argovitz said that Dickey would not be available for an interview, offering up some lame excuse. I had been had—screwed by a crazy dentist posing as a reputable sports agent. There was nothing I could do at that point, but I vowed that I would have my revenge.

We flew to Bryan, Texas, in Argovitz's helicopter and got pictures of Dickey's "shack" of a home, where he had grown up with five brothers. The footage of the neighborhood, to say the least, was compelling. We returned later that day to Jerry's office in Houston and sat down for an interview. Dr. Argovitz was in for a shock. He was expecting a sympathetic interview about the poverty-stricken childhood of Curtis Dickey. I turned the guns on him.

I asked him if he had ever stepped foot inside that home. Had he taken the time to get to know Dickey's mother and family? Had he even met them? Of course he had not. I then asked Argovitz how he could play God with a young man's life without knowing anything about him. Jerry was not happy with my line of questioning, but of course I was thrilled with the interview.

The piece aired the following Sunday night, and the reaction from both the public and media members was very complimentary.

## ❖ One More Dickey Dilemma

The Colts 1981 season started with a one-point victory over the New England Patriots, and then the wheels came off. They suffered an eight-game losing streak, and the team reached a new low when they hosted the New York Jets on November 8 of that year.

During the early first quarter, Curtis Dickey fumbled a handoff. The Jets recovered and kicked a field goal. On the Colts' next possession, quarterback Bert Jones had to scramble on third down and was tackled for a loss. Jones got up, shouting at Dickey and waving his arms in a show of anger. The entire stadium was a witness to Jones's verbal onslaught.

After the game, Bert explained to the media what he was saying to Dickey: "Don't just stand there when I'm scrambling. Come back to me. Block somebody, do something to make a play." To make matters worse, Jones's frustration was further demonstrated when he told the media that Dickey had fallen asleep several times during team meetings.

One of the players after the game told me that Curtis had accused Jones of racism, but the player said he would not say that to me on camera. The next day following practice, I waited for Dickey to get dressed and confronted him as he was leaving the locker room. I asked Dickey point blank if he thought Bert Jones was a racist. Without hesitation, he said yes.

I continued to ask questions about his relationship with Jones, and Dickey said he knew of several other former players who had racial disagreements with Bert. I couldn't believe what Dickey was telling me, but I knew I had one hell of a damaging interview.

When I got back to the TV station, I called Colts GM Ernie Accorsi and told him he needed to watch the six o'clock sports (I was now doing both the six and eleven o'clock newscasts). When the Dickey interview aired, the Colts season went from tragedy to turmoil and became an ugly national headline.

WMAR was the CBS affiliate in Baltimore, and the next day Bryant Gumbel called me to say he wanted Dickey's interview for their Sunday show *NFL Today*.

The next day at the Colts complex, Bert Jones confronted me after practice, highly upset, saying I used "dirty" interview tactics. He said he would never talk to me again, and as far as he was concerned, I could go to hell.

Thirty-one years later, I still haven't talked to Bert Jones.

### ❖ 280 Park Avenue

Colts GM Ernie Accorsi and I were talking one day in his office about NFL commissioner Pete Rozelle and the job he was doing as the league's top guy. Ernie said that if I was interested in going to New York for a sit-down interview with the commish he could set it up. I jumped at the chance, and several weeks later I walked into NFL headquarters at 280 Park Avenue in Manhattan.

Rozelle's rise to power was neither predicted nor expected. In fact, Rozelle was a compromise choice in 1960 after seven days of haggling. Pete was selected on the twenty-third ballot by the owners, who thought the thirty-three-year-old kid from California could easily be controlled. But the owners greatly underestimated the former Los Angeles Rams public relations director. His accomplishments as commissioner became legendary, and his impact on the league continues today.

My photographer and I were ushered into the commissioner's lavish conference room, where we set up our equipment and waited for him to arrive.

At one end of the room, I saw large boxes stacked on top of each other. I wandered over to get a closer look, and to my surprise I saw boxes stamped with team names. Inside were Super Bowl tickets.

When the commissioner came in for the interview, I questioned him about the tickets, and he said he would be glad when they were distributed because he was tired of worrying about their safety. We had a good laugh, and talked for the next thirty minutes about his career and the business of the NFL. The most fascinating part of the interview was listening to him describe his interaction with the unique and diverse personalities of the league owners.

## ❖ Who Is This Kid?

Ernie Accorsi, Colts GM, told me about a "wonder kid" in Baltimore who knew absolutely everything about each of the players who would be drafted by the NFL that April. Ernie suggested I do a story with him, because the kid was uncanny and unusual in his ability to analyze players and rank them according to their talent level and probability to help a team.

The kid attended Calvert High School, and I understood that he'd never played a down of football his entire life. I called him up, and he invited me to his home. His name was Mel Kiper Jr.

When I arrived, I was met by a skinny kid who didn't look a day over sixteen. He took me downstairs to the basement, and I couldn't believe my eyes. I had never seen so many videotapes in my life. Not even at a TV station. They were tapes of college football games from several years back to the present. He even had practice video of players. There were stacks of papers everywhere with detailed information and stats about each player.

A Baltimore Blast

Mel did his first draft book in 1979 and sent it to all the GMs in the league, just to see what they thought. He was especially proud of the encouraging responses from Don Shula and Bill Walsh.

Kiper told me that ever since childhood, sports had been his passion. He said all he thought about was sports, especially football. He understood early on that football was all about technique and discovered that he had an analytical mind for the game. He talked a mile a minute that day . . . just as he does now as the guru of the NFL draft for ESPN.

Mel was attending Essex Community College, but his heart was in this new business venture. His parents agreed, and the rest is NFL history.

I was the first person to put Mel Kiper Jr. on TV and the first to offer him a job on draft day (without pay). When April rolled around, I invited Mel to come to the station, and together we watched the NFL draft (first televised on ESPN in 1980). Mel would comment on the players taken in the first round, and we videotaped our discussion for a Sunday night draft show. Mel, of course, was a hit, and, with Ernie Accorsi's help, I had discovered the wonder kid from Baltimore.

One of the items I have held onto over the years is a copy of *The 1982 Draft Report*, by Mel Kiper Jr., Sports Analyst—Winline Sports Service, Inc. On the cover is quarterback Jim McMahon of Brigham Young.

Here's what Kiper said about Mike Munchak, whom he ranked number two in the '82 draft among offensive guards, behind teammate Sean Farrell of Penn State:

> Missed the 1980 season with knee surgery, but came back strong in 1981 and had an outstanding year. Showed marked improvement from game to game and by the latter part of the season was grading out as high as his heralded teammate Sean Farrell. Extremely aggressive and is very explosive at the point of attack—outstanding one-on-one blocker and rarely beaten in pass protection. An underrated player who was over-shadowed by the accomplishments of Farrell, but has the ability to be one of the top players at his position in the N.F.L.

In Hines' Sight

Munchak was the eighth overall pick in the '82 draft by the Houston Oilers and had an eleven-year Hall of Fame career, all with the Oilers. Now, of course, he is head coach of the Tennessee Titans.

## ❖ The Man Everybody Loved to Hate

"Arrogant, pompous, obnoxious, vain, cruel, verbose, a showoff. I have been called all of these. Of course I am," said the late *How-wuuuud Co-sellll*. The way he pronounced his name dripped with chutzpah and unabashed self-promotion. In his day, Howard Cosell was arguably the most mimicked and mocked man in America. Those negative attributes, however, were balanced almost equally by his intelligence and ability to entertain.

Howard's biography notes:

> Despite obvious drawbacks—a nasal Brooklyn accent, an obvious toupee, and a propensity for prolix pronouncements—Howard Cosell changed the face and voice of sports broadcasting forever, replacing bland, sycophantic, sanitized commentary with hard-nosed observations and often unpopular stands of principle. All of which contributed to him being loved and hated in almost equal measure.

I became a Howard Cosell fan the first time I saw him on television sometime in the late 1960s. Howard was the "spark" that fired the original *Monday Night Football* broadcast team on ABC beginning in 1970. In the booth with Cosell were Frank Gifford and "Dandy" Don Meredith.

Another *Monday Night* icon, Al Michaels, said about Cosell: "History will reflect that Howard Cosell was easily the dominant sportscaster of all time."

My first meeting with Howard happened in Baltimore. He was in town to broadcast the Preakness for ABC, and I had arranged to do a sit-down interview with him during the early part of Preakness week. I showed up at his hotel the morning of the scheduled interview, and I was a nervous wreck. The man was my hero, and I knew there was no way I could come close to meeting the career standards he had set as an interviewer.

He arrived almost thirty minutes late, which only added to my heightened anxiety. I can honestly say I was fearful, fretful, afraid, and fidgety. I have never—before or since—experienced those emotions when facing an interview.

Howard could not have been warmer in his greeting. He seemed like the complete opposite of "Howard the Huge TV Personality" that many people loved to hate. I don't remember a thing we talked about, but I will never forget how engaging he was following the interview. He was genuinely interested in my career, and we talked at some length about sportscasting and television in general.

Maybe he was just being polite when he said to me, "If I can ever be of help to you, don't hesitate to call me." He looked and sounded sincere, and as he held out his hand to shake, I almost felt like I should kiss his ring instead.

The following Friday evening was the annual gala dinner party for the Preakness. Pat and I attended and made our way to the open bar, where Cosell was having a drink (make that several). I had told Pat about my meeting and interview with Howard, and she was just as anxious to meet him.

Howard was by himself at the time and seemed delighted when Pat and I joined him at the bar. I introduced Pat, and immediately, Howard—in a low, hushed Brooklyn voice as only Howard could—looked directly into her face and said, "Such beauty, and what a lovely, succulent lower lip you have, my dear."

Howard's charm stunned Pat like a surprise birthday party. She and I looked at each other, then at Howard, and we burst out laughing. By now others had begun to form a circle around us, and for the next half hour we were entertained by the former host of ABC's *Saturday Night Live with Howard Cosell.*

In a 1995 article in the *Washington Post*, Shirley Povich wrote, "If there was a defining reaction to Howard Cosell by the sportswriters he castigated so often as 'utterly obnoxious,' it was probably delivered by the late and beloved Red Smith. With his characteristic subtlety it was Red who once said, 'I have tried hard to like Howard Cosell, and I have failed.'"

My late friend, syndicated columnist Lewis Grizzard, wrote, "Very few people liked Howard Cosell . . . but that's the point.

America learned to love to hate Howard, and once he left the broadcast to pretenders, the broadcast became deathly dull."

## ❖ An Incomplete Spring Training

Life doesn't get any better than going from winter sweaters and coats to short sleeves at spring training. That's the way I felt in late February arriving in Miami for Orioles spring training in 1982.

It had been a tough winter in Baltimore, and I welcomed the sun, the soft breezes, and the other scenery Miami had to offer. Spring training was a happy time. The players were in a good mood, and there was almost a giddy atmosphere in camp that year. It would be manager Earl Weaver's last year to manage the birds, and everybody was talking and writing about the story of his final season.

The Orioles held spring training at Miami Stadium on Tenth Avenue, in a run-down section of town. Everyone (players, officials, media, fans) had been warned not to park their cars near the stadium. Just a few days before camp, pitcher Sammy Stewart had purchased a 1982 red and white Cadillac, which he unwisely parked right next to the players' entrance. Headed back to his car following a morning workout, he froze in his tracks, not believing what he was seeing. His brand-new Caddy was jacked up on blocks with all four tires and wheels missing. As a joke, several of the players took up a locker room collection so Sammy could buy a "junk" car in keeping with the neighborhood.

Earlier in the week, I had interviewed Orioles owner Edward Bennett Williams, a prominent and ultra-successful Washington, D.C., defense attorney. Williams was a man not given to interviews, but he had agreed to sit for our Sunday night magazine show. Williams's clients had included Frank Sinatra, John Hinckley Jr., Playboy publisher Hugh Hefner, spy Igor Melekh, Jimmy Hoffa, organized crime figure Frank Costello, and Senator Joseph McCarthy, among others. Williams was also part owner and president of the Washington Redskins. Williams died in 1988. He once said, "I will defend anyone as long as the client gives me total control of the case and pays up front."

Late one afternoon in early March, still in Miami at training camp, I got a phone call from WMAR news anchor Tom Sweeney. Tom informed me that the negotiations between station management and the American Federation of Television and Radio Artists (AFTRA) had broken down, and all of the station's on-air talent, except one, was going on strike. With urgency in his voice, Tom said I needed to get on a plane and get back to Baltimore immediately.

The next two months were eight weeks of high anxiety among the twenty-plus of us who went on strike. We had the support of the Teamsters, the Communication Workers of America, and other local unions, which picketed the station's offices on York Road. We were a band of dysfunctional anchors and reporters trying to hold our lives and careers together. I witnessed grown men crying and pleading with the group to vote to settle the strike so we could all get back to work.

Oprah Winfrey, who had left Nashville several years before I arrived in Baltimore, was cohosting a talk show on WJZ-TV, the ABC affiliate. Oprah joined us on the picket line several times along with other local anchors and reporters from competing stations, as a show of support.

My two-year contract with WMAR ran out during the strike, and station manager Ernie Kliner called saying he wanted me to sign another contract. I thanked him for the offer but told him I couldn't. Of course he knew why. If I signed a new deal and crossed the picket line, I would be considered a strike breaker, a scab. If I ever wanted to work at another union station, I could never cross the picket line, so I didn't.

Many of us on strike tried to pick up any job we could to help pay the bills. The movie *Best Friends*, starring Burt Reynolds and Goldie Hawn, was being filmed in Washington, and I went on a "cattle call" for extras in a scene they were shooting at the Georgetown Plaza. The movie was directed by Norman Jewison and cowritten by Baltimore native Barry Levinson. I worked two days on the set, spending 98 percent of that time sitting around drinking coffee and reading. I probably didn't pocket enough money to buy a nice dinner, but what the heck . . . I was working on a movie, and now I have written about it.

After eight long, grueling weeks, the strike was finally settled and we went back to work. But relationships between station management and many of the strikers had been permanently damaged, and it was just never the same.

In Hines' Sight

By late summer, the bad blood between management and strikers was so bad that most had left or been fired. Management was determined to start over with new talent, and I found myself walking again . . . out the door.

## ❖ A Novel Period

I spent the next few weeks reflecting on my life and career and the possibilities for the future. And then I made a decision. I would do nothing for the next few months as I tried to get my head on straight. I talked it over with Pat, and she agreed.

I had just been through perhaps the worst stretch of time in my life, and I wanted to do something radical. So I did two things. I was already a jogger, but I took my running to a higher level and started running five to eight miles four times a week for an average of about thirty miles a week. I also started writing a book . . . a romance novel. Now that's what you call . . . radical.

Here's the background story. A romance novelist appeared on a talk show at WMAR one day, and I just happened to be watching as she talked about how many romance novels she had written and the millions she had sold over the years. As I listened, I thought, I can do that. And that's where the idea was born. I now had the time, and I decided to go for it. It was 180 degrees from anything I had ever done, and the challenge drove me.

Running and writing became my life. I went out and bought at least ten romance novels (only my wife knew) and studied the formula for writing in that genre. In December, I mailed a copy of *Love on the Run* to Harlequin books, and then I waited.

Six months later, I received a rejection letter (which I still have) that said, in part: "Your manuscript was read by several editors, and although reports were varied, there was not sufficient enthusiasm to allow us to publish." It was signed by Jennifer Campbell, senior editor. (By the way, the letter was addressed to "Ms. Hope Hines.")

Mission accomplished as far as I was concerned. Yes, I was disappointed they didn't want to publish it, but at least it had been read, and I had even gotten a reply from a senior editor. The challenge had been completed, and it was time to move on to whatever was next.

What happened next was that my wife turned to me one day and said, "Hope, it's time we went back to Nashville."

"Well, okaaaaay," I said. "I didn't have anything better planned. Sure, why not?" What I was going to do when I got to Nashville? I had no idea.

## In Hines' Sight

In just over a decade I had experienced glorious highs and depressing lows in television. We all get knocked down in our journey through this life, and I was beginning to clearly understand that what happens to you is not as important as how you react to what happens. Writing that romance novel, I was able to turn a negative situation, being jobless, into a challenging, stimulating pursuit, proving you can do anything as long as you want it badly enough and you never give up. You could argue that it was not a success since it wasn't published, and you would be correct. But as far as I was concerned, completing what I set out to do and then having it reviewed, by a major publisher, was victory enough for me.

Working in Baltimore was one of the great experiences of my life. Pat and Danny loved it as much as I did. It is a wonderful city with very passionate sports fans. We still have friends there, and we will always be a fan of the city and the Orioles. The area reminded us so much of Nashville, with its rolling hills. We loved the Inner Harbor, with its restaurants and beautiful scenery; crab dinners with friends at neighborhood bars; trips to Washington, D.C.; train rides to New York for a weekend Broadway play; Sunday drives to Annapolis; and eating peanuts and watching the Orioles at Memorial Stadium. And of course, we loved to entertain family and friends who came to visit.

# 9

# Going Home Again

## NASHVILLE 1983–1988

I T WAS TIME TO "U-HAUL-IT" to Nashville again, and something told me this would be our final destination. Within days of arriving back in Music City, I called Tom Ervin, station manager at WTVF, described what had happened in Baltimore, and told him I had moved back to Nashville.

"Tom," I said, "I don't know what your situation is relative to a sports anchor, or if you have any openings at all, but if you would like to talk with me, I would certainly like to discuss with you any possibilities that exist at Channel 5. Tom immediately said he would like to meet and we arranged a time.

I parked in front of Channel 5 on James Robertson Parkway and thought about how surreal this was. Eight years had passed since I walked out of the station in December 1975. Memories of San Diego, New Orleans, Tallahassee, Charlotte, and Baltimore flooded my thoughts. I bowed my head. "Lord, your will be done, but I certainly would like to work here again, so I place myself in your hands and will praise you no matter the outcome." I was at peace as I walked through the doors of Channel 5 to find out if I really could . . . come home again. Tom Ervin later described the scene in his office:

Our receptionist called me to say Hope Hines was here to see me. I jumped up and met him when he entered my office. We hugged, and I said, "Welcome home, Hope."

I brought some video of my work from Baltimore to my meeting with Tom, but he winked and said, "I think I'm familiar with your work, Hope." Then he got down to business. "Bill Swanbeck is our main sports anchor. He's under contract for another year. Tony Troiano is our weekend sports anchor. If you are willing to anchor the weekend and report during the week, I'll move Tony to a weekday reporter. If things go like I think they will, you will become sports director again."

I worked the next six months or so as the weekend sports anchor, and true to his word, Tom made the change.

You certainly can go home again. Sorry, Thomas Wolfe.

> Listen close and you shall hear
> The whispering wind both
> Far and near.
> Truths revealed while all alone
> That you might find the way
> Back home
>
> —Daniel

## ❖ Death of a Salesman

One of the first people I visited after returning to Channel 5 was John Merritt. John was ill and spent most of his time at home with Maxine, his wife. Big John had been a long-time diabetic, and the disease was taking a heavy toll on his body. When I walked in his house and saw him sitting in his big easy chair in a robe and pajamas, I was shocked. Gone was the vibrancy, exuberance, and enthusiasm he'd always had. He looked haggard, gaunt, and emaciated. He had been in and out of the hospital several times the past few months, and his prognosis was not good.

By early December, family, friends, and former players were being told Coach Merritt probably wouldn't make it to Christmas. John Merritt died December 13, 1983. It snowed the day of his funeral. A who's who of former players, city leaders, politicians, and business owners packed the church that day. I was privileged to be included among the honorary pall-bearers.

Coach Merritt left behind a coaching legacy that will likely never be equaled at Tennessee State in terms of wins and longevity. The school plays the John Merritt Classic each year to honor the coach who won four undisputed national championships among historically black colleges. The city of Nashville named John A. Merritt Boulevard in his honor in 1982.

One more John Merritt story, before I pass him off to history: Big John loved to tell about the recruiting trip he and "Shorty" (John's personal driver) took to Wrightsville, Georgia, in 1980. John knew his chances of landing a young man by the name of Herschel Walker were slim, but he went anyway. With Shorty driving, Big John's Cadillac turned onto a dirt road that led up a hill to Walker's home. Halfway to the house Merritt said, "Stop the car, Shorty. Ain't no use going any further."

"What do you mean, Coach?" Shorty said, slamming on the brakes.

"See that bright-red Trans-Am? Georgia has already got 'im. Turn the car around and let's go home."

John would always laugh out loud as he finished the story. "Yeah, I had something for Herschel too, but hell, a Trans-Am will beat a dozen loaves of Bunny Bread everyday."

## In Hines' Sight

I learned from John Merritt what late Yankees owner George Steinbrenner is credited with saying: "Always surround yourself with people who are a lot smarter than you are."

David Ogilvy, regarded as the founding father of modern advertising, said, "If you ever find a man who is better than you are . . . hire him. If necessary, pay him more than you would pay yourself."

That's what John did. He found assistant coaches who were smarter and more knowledgeable than he was and hired them. Merritt had the ability to get everyone in his organization to believe in his ability to diagram a winning course of action that resulted in everyone sharing in the fortune.

Coach Merritt always thought of himself as a part-time coach and a full-time salesman. Day and night he sold Tennessee State University and his football program to anyone who would listen. Tens of thousands listened and gladly bought his product.

Successful businessman Alan Keith said, "Leadership is ultimately about creating a way for people to contribute to making something extraordinary happen." With John Merritt, something extraordinary was always happening.

## ❖ The Flying Putter

During the mid '80s, Vanderbilt basketball coach C. M. Newton held an annual charity golf tournament each summer and invited numerous coaching pals. One of those who made an appearance every year was his good friend Bobby Knight, head coach of the Indiana Hoosiers.

This particular year, my photographer, Michael Redd, was shooting Knight as he was putting out on his final hole. As Bobby was about to putt, he stopped and instructed Michael and me to move. We were standing in his line of sight behind the green. Once we had moved, Knight addressed the ball and putted, missing the hole by two feet. It was at that moment his putter went airborne, just missing the two of us as we jumped out of the way. "The black guy made me miss," Knight said to no one in particular as he retrieved his putter.

I had asked for a one-on-one interview with Knight upon completion of his round, but I now doubted he would honor that. But shortly he walked over and said, "I shouldn't talk to you, but what the hell. I guess I owe you. Turn the damn camera on and let's do it." His reputation for having an irritable disposition was well deserved.

Knight didn't like my first question, and he gave me a "smartass" Bobby Knight answer. He didn't like my second question either, so he butted in and said, "Hold it. I'm done with you." Then he shouted to C. M., who was standing nearby, "I thought you said this guy was okay to talk to. He's asking me one dumb-ass question after another." Knight was on stage now and doing what he does best ∴ . . trying to intimidate a reporter.

I don't remember the questions that riled Bobby, but his responses were going to make for some really good TV, and I was

*Above:* Boots Donnelly, former Middle Tennessee State head football coach, and Vince Gill on the links with Danny and me, 1998. *Right:* With boxing promoter Don King in the late 1990s. *Below:* With former Alabama and New York Jets Super Bowl–winning quarterback Joe Namath, 2005.

The late Walter Payton, Chicago Bears running back, member of the 1985 winning Super Bowl team, and NFL Hall of Famer.

*Back row (l–r):* Mark Howard, Bob Kusek, Neil O'Donnell; *front row:* Brian McKeegan, me, Eric Yutzy, mid 2000s.

*Below:* Boarding DW's plane for Indianapolis with Gordon Inman, Darrell Waltrip, Tim Pagliara, Melvin Spain, and John Gallagher, 2008.

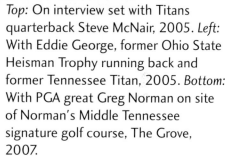

*Top:* On interview set with Titans quarterback Steve McNair, 2005. *Left:* With Eddie George, former Ohio State Heisman Trophy running back and former Tennessee Titan, 2005. *Bottom:* With PGA great Greg Norman on site of Norman's Middle Tennessee signature golf course, The Grove, 2007.

With Danny at my surprise
60th birthday party.

Brian McKeegan, NewsChannel 5
sports producer and photographer,
and Bob Kusek, 2011.

I was the emcee at a benefit dinner
honoring country music superstar
Faith Hill at the Country Music Hall of
Fame, 2004.

Scenes from my July 2011 retirement party *(top to bottom)*: John Majors, former Pittsburgh National Champion coach and University of Tennessee head coach, speaks to the crowd; Vince Gill, Mark Howard, George Plaster, and Bill Anderson; sharing a laugh with Darrell Waltrip, Vince Gill, and Bill Anderson.

Tom Ervin, former NewsChannel 5 station manager, and Harry Chapman, long-time Channel 5 personality.

With Brad Hopkins, former Titan All-Pro left tackle.

With the Boomers Bible study group: Mike Arrington, Dr. Bryant Millsaps, me, David Miller, Pete Kutz, Rob McDonald, Ted Bleymaier.

*Top left:* Fishing with grandsons Ryan and Jack Hines, 2010. *Top right:* NewsChannel 5 2010 Christmas card, with Ron Howes, Chris Clark, Vickie Yates, Rory Johnson, and Kristin Priesol. *Bottom:* My daughter, Donna Hatton, with her husband, Paige, and their daughters, Julianne and Jordan.

My son Lyman Hines and his wife, Jill, with their sons, Ryan and Jack.

My son Danny Pennington and his daughter, Addie.

*Right:* Former Channel 5 director Jimmy Bewley, to whom I said so many times, "Roll the tape, J.B."
*Below:* The staff at the Brentwood Waffle House put up a plaque in my honor that says "In Hines Sight."
*Left to right,* Tammy Farris, Mel Stovall, Daniel Trujillo, Mike Wise, Kaye Alcorn, Lynda Cawthon.

pleased with what we were getting on camera for all to see. C. M. understood what was happening and came over in the name of good PR to smooth Knight's feathers. Newton urged him to continue with the interview while asking me to begin again with another line of questioning. We both agreed, but Bobby had one more trick up his sleeve.

Michael was shooting the interview with the camera on his shoulder. As we continued, what the audience could not see was Bobby repeatedly tapping Michael's crotch with his putter. He poked him every ten seconds or so. Ever the consummate pro, Michael continued to do his job as if nothing out of the ordinary was happening. When the interview was over, Knight walked away as if he had just conducted a normal, everyday interview.

"Bobby Knight is crazy!" Michael said, with a look of disbelief and urgent agitation in his voice. I broke out laughing and put my arm around his shoulders. "Michael," I said, "you are a special guy."

"Special? What's so special about being poked in the crotch with a putter?"

"Because," I said, "you have just been 'knighted' by the king of scorn. Plus you have a personal Bobby Knight story you can recount time and time again, year after year, and believe me . . . it will never get old."

It was my pleasure—or displeasure, depending on his mood— to interview Bobby Knight several times over the years. But that day on the golf course is a special memory, as I was involved in one of the most bizarre interview scenes of my career.

### ❖ Doc Gets a Second Chance

Sometime in the early part of 1986, highly successful and popular Middle Tennessee State University head football coach Boots Donnelly had made up his mind. Doc Kreis deserved a second chance.

On April 20, 1985, E. J. "Doc" Kreis resigned as Vanderbilt's strength coach. Six months later, on November 27, Doc was sentenced to one year's probation for his part in participating in a scheme to distribute ninety-seven thousand doses of steroids and other prescription drugs to athletes at three universities. Investigators said most of the doses went to athletes who gathered at "Doc's Body Shop," otherwise known as the Vanderbilt weight room. Five to six thousand went to Clemson, and about seventeen hundred doses went to Colgate.

The scandal shook Vanderbilt like an earthquake that measured eight on the Richter scale. Doc was one of the most beloved figures in the history of Vanderbilt athletics, which made his involvement in the wrongdoing even more painful for all concerned.

Coach Donnelly needed a strength coach. Doc needed a job. Donnelly also knew no one would touch Doc because of his misconduct, but Doc was one of the best in the business, and Donnelly wanted to give him a second chance. Boots clearly had a dilemma and needed a plan. If he wanted to hire Doc, whose life and career had been shredded by steroids, Donnelly would have to eliminate the possibility of any bad publicity. He also knew his idea had potential for disaster.

Boots met with John Bibb, sports editor of the *Tennessean*, and told him of his desire to give Doc a second chance. He asked Bibb for help. Bibb told Boots he was crazy, but if he was dead set on hiring Doc (Bibb was a Doc fan), he would write a favorable article. However, first they needed to meet with John Seigenthaler, publisher (later chairman) of the *Tennessean*.

Seigenthaler had been Boots's baseball coach in grade school, and the two had a lifelong relationship. Seigenthaler patiently listened to Boots plead his case and then, with agitated anger in his voice, he said, "Boots, if you do this . . . you will destroy your career."

Donnelly persisted, telling Seigenthaler, "John, I really need Doc and Doc needs me. It's the right thing to do."

Seigenthaler could see he was beaten. Nobody said a word while the distinguished publisher was deep in thought. He suddenly threw up his hands in surrender, breaking the silence with, "Okay, Boots if you're so determined this is a good thing for both you and Doc, the paper will back you. Hell, we'll 'canonize' him. How's that?"

Then Boots said, "Gentlemen, for this to work, and to be certain there will be no adverse publicity, I need to give the story to Joe Biddle of the *Banner* (the afternoon newspaper). Remember, you guys broke the original story of Doc's involvement with steroids, beating Joe and the *Banner*, and if I don't give this story to Joe, I'm afraid he will kill Doc in his column."

That bit of news, to say the least, was unsettling to Seigenthaler and Bibb. Donnelly explained that he would arrange a meeting with Biddle to see if he would go along with the "no bad publicity" angle before any decision was made, again asking Seigenthaler and Bibb to go along with his scheme.

Boots met with Biddle and explained that the only way he could make his plan to hire Doc Kreis work was if Joe would agree to write something positive about Doc and not crucify him in the *Banner*.

Biddle listened with sympathy. Then he told Boots there was no way he would write a favorable article about Doc, but he wouldn't do anything to hurt Doc either. Therefore, he wouldn't write anything at all.

Biddle explained to Donnelly that he had the steroid story before the *Tennessean* had first broken it, and he had gone to Vanderbilt football coach George MacIntyre that morning to question him. MacIntyre told Biddle he didn't know anything about it and asked Joe to wait in his office, saying there was something he had to do, and left Joe alone.

Biddle waited for over an hour, and then Doc and his attorney Roger May walked into MacIntyre's office. They told Biddle there would be no comments about the story. By then, Biddle's deadline for the afternoon paper had passed and he missed breaking the story, which meant Joe had been screwed. He would forever hold a grudge.

Donnelly's plan was crystallizing, but several important pieces needed to fall into place first. He met with school president Dr. Sam Ingram and presented his idea.

"No, you will not do that on my watch," Ingram said, with an icy cold stare.

Boots had gotten too far with his scheme to have it derailed now. "Dr. Ingram, if you'll go along with me on this . . . I'll make you a hero. I promise." Boots then explained that he wanted to put Doc in high schools all over middle Tennessee to talk about the dangers of using steroids, putting a positive spin on the horrible mistake he had made. Dr. Ingram finally gave his blessing, but with this warning, "There better not be one negative word about Middle Tennessee in any of this."

With his marching orders from Dr. Ingram, Boots called his good friend Fred Pancoast, the former Vanderbilt head football coach, to solicit his help. Pancoast was a recovering alcoholic. Boots explained his plan to hire Doc and asked Pancoast if he would be willing to partner with Doc to speak at high schools in the area about the evils of drugs and alcohol. Pancoast agreed.

The next phone call Boots made was . . . to me. "Hope, how would you like to have the first exclusive interview with Doc Kreis?" Up until that point, during all the months of investigation and trial, Doc had not talked to anyone in the media about his involvement in the steroid scandal, and of course I jumped at the opportunity.

I understood completely what Boots hoped to accomplish with the interview I would conduct with Doc. I had a very good relationship with Boots, but I told him I would have to ask hard, probing questions, and there could be no stipulations on the interview whatsoever. He agreed and asked if I would include Pancoast in the interview with Doc, and I agreed.

Doc Kreis couldn't have been more open and transparent during our interview. People witnessed a very humble and contrite human being, and it turned out to be an interview I was very proud of.

Several weeks after our interview aired on Channel 5, Doc wrote a letter thanking me for the manner in which I conducted the interview and included a poem by Ella Wheeler Wilcox, "Two Kinds of People." I still have the framed poem and Doc's letter.

I also included Fred Pancoast in portions of the Doc Kreis interview. Not only did Fred once have a drinking problem, he had been addicted to Valium as well. After the camera was turned off, Fred looked at me and said with a deadpan expression, "Thanks, Hope. Now everybody will think I am a drunk." We both had a good laugh.

Boots had one more major obstacle to clear before he could hire Doc. There was no money in the MTSU athletic budget to pay for a strength coach. So Boots called Al Phillips, a Nashville insurance executive, along with several Vanderbilt and Doc supporters, to a meeting at Hillwood country club.

Boots told the group how much money it would take to hire Doc for two years and asked if they wanted to help him get a second chance. He said the money would have to be in the bank by a certain date or there would be no deal.

They got the money, and on August 21, 1986, it was announced that Doc Kreis, the former Vanderbilt strength coach who resigned after he became the central figure in the steroid scandal that rocked the university and other schools, had been named strength coach for the Middle Tennessee State University football team.

Boots Donnelly had used all of the skills he had acquired as a head football coach and diagramed the perfect strategy for getting what he needed: a strength coach. At the same time, he resurrected Doc Kreis from the heap of ridicule and scorn. I was proud to have played a small role in that process.

## In Hines' Sight

Sometimes in this life, before we are called to offer someone a second chance, we must first take a chance ourselves. Sadly, too few among us are willing to put it on the line for someone else, even when it's the right thing to do. It takes someone with an uncommon heart, someone who understands that the reward will almost always exceed the risk, and someone who understands that the boldest decisions, made with conviction, are the safest.

Someone once said, "Life is too short to wake up with regrets. So love the people who treat you right. Forget about the ones who don't. Believe things happen for a reason. If you get a second chance, grab it with both hands. If it changes your life, let it. Nobody said life would be easy, they just promised it would be worth it."

### ❖ Brown for Black & Gold

One of the casualties of the turmoil during that 1985 Vanderbilt football season was coach George MacIntyre, who resigned after seven seasons as head coach with a record of 25-52-1. Despite his record, MacIntyre was one of the most respected coaches in college football, but the steroid embarrassment, plus a final season that produced only three wins, was enough for Coach Mac. He stepped down in December.

Vanderbilt athletic director Roy Kramer had to find a replacement for MacIntyre. Thirty-six-year-old Watson Brown was his choice. Watson seemed to be the perfect match for the Commodores. He was a native of Cookeville, Tennessee, and a four-year starter at quarterback for Vandy, and he had also been offensive coordinator under MacIntyre in '81 and '82 before successive head coaching jobs at Cincinnati and Rice.

Kramer held Watson's press conference in the press box at Vanderbilt stadium with an overflow crowd in attendance. It was assumed by the Vanderbilt faithful that Watson Brown would produce a winning football program. But their exuberance was short lived. Five years later, Brown had won just ten games, which included three 1–10 seasons.

In 1990, Roy Kramer left Vanderbilt to become commissioner of the Southeastern Conference, and Paul Hoolahan was hired as his replacement.

The Commodore nation was not prepared for what happened in the opening game of 1990. SMU had just returned from two years of college football exile, known as the "death penalty," for recruiting violations. The Mustangs embarrassed Vanderbilt in Dallas 44–7.

The Watson Brown era had reached a definite low point, and there were immediate whispers of his demise. The following week, Brown rallied his team and they beat LSU. Then came eight straight loses. Only one game remained. Vandy would host Tennessee, and the season couldn't come to a close soon enough for some supporters. Watson, however, remained popular with most fans.

Several weeks before the Vandy-Tennessee game, I had a source deep within the Vanderbilt athletic department telling me they were certain Paul Hoolahan was going to fire Watson very quickly after the Vandy-UT game. I had known and trusted this person for many years and had no reason whatsoever to doubt the truth of this tip. But before I went on the air with the story, I had to try to find another source who could confirm what I had been told. I couldn't. There was only one thing left for me to do.

On the Monday before the Vanderbilt-Tennessee game, I called Paul Hoolahan's office for an appointment. His secretary called back and said he could meet with me on Tuesday morning.

"Paul," I said as our meeting began, "I'm going to ask you to help me with something. I know you are going to fire Watson sometime this weekend, and I am going to break the story today. If the story is incorrect . . . tell me not to do it."

Paul smiled and leaned forward on his desk. "You're on your own, Hope. You'll just have to roll the dice. I'm not going to help you one way or the other." I left his office with my stomach in a knot. I checked with my source one more time and was assured it would happen. "Okay," I said, "I am placing my reputation in your hands, and on your word I'm breaking the story tonight at six."

I was told by my source, with conviction, "Go for it. You won't be sorry. I promise."

When I got to the station I tried to call Watson and tell him I was going on the air at six o'clock with the story that he would be fired following the Tennessee game, but I couldn't get in touch with him. I knew that that afternoon, after practice, he would be speaking at the weekly meeting of the Commodore Club, so I told weekend anchor and reporter Mark Howard to take Bob Kusek, our sports photographer, and go to the meeting and ask Watson if he had any indication he would be fired following the Tennessee game. I also told Mark to tell Watson I was breaking the story at six and that I had tried to get him on the phone but couldn't. I didn't want him to be blindsided by the story.

When Mark asked if he had had any warning he would be fired following the Tennessee game, Watson became visibly upset and angry with Mark for asking the question. He said he had no indication whatsoever from Paul Hoolahan or anyone else he would be fired, and the only thing he was worried about was beating Tennessee on Saturday. At six o'clock, I said I had learned from a very reliable source within the athletic department that Watson would be fired the following weekend. I then aired Brown's soundbite, in its entirety.

By the time I got off the set and walked to the newsroom, the phones were blazing. Callers were livid over my prophecy. Even with his record, Watson continued to be very popular with fans, and it seemed everyone wanted to run me out of town for the way I had treated him.

I had pulled the trigger on the story and would die many times in the next five days waiting for Saturday's game.

The other media outlets didn't touch the story, because they didn't have any sources who could confirm what I had been told, so they didn't do anything, but they were nervous. After the six o'clock news on Wednesday, the next day, I got a call from Paul Hoolahan. I had done the Watson Brown story again, with some additional information. When I answered the phone, Paul said, "How does it feel, out there on a limb all alone?"

"Not too bad," I responded, surprised that he would call. "Why don't you cut me some slack, Paul, and confirm what I've reported is true."

"Not on your life, Bucko. I'm going to let you twist in the wind. But I must say I do admire your nerve," and he hung up.

About midnight, my phone rang at home. I answered. It was Paul Hoolahan again. I quickly suspected he had tossed back a couple of late night cocktails. At first he asked who my source was for the story. Next he demanded I tell him. Then when I wouldn't, he hung up. That phone call told me all I needed to know. Paul had not counted on the story getting out until after the Tennessee game, and he didn't like it one bit that I had jumped the gun.

I was later told that the rest of that week was quite tense around McGugin Center. John Bibb of the *Tennessean* took me to task, questioning the authenticity of the report and saying it was highly unlikely that the well-liked Brown would be fired.

Watson's post-game press conference following Vandy's 49–20 loss to Tennessee was packed with reporters and photographers. He might as well have been facing a firing squad. When asked if he was going to be fired, he pointed to Paul Hoolahan, who was standing in the back of the room, and said, "Ask him." And with that, the press conference was over. Watson walked out one door and Hoolahan the other.

Larry Woody, former Vanderbilt beat writer for the *Tennessean*, followed Hoolahan outside to get a quote, but the Vandy AD was already being confronted by Watson's wife Brenda, who was in his face. A Vanderbilt assistant coach stepped between them and led Brenda away.

On Sunday, Hoolahan called a press conference to announce that Watson Brown had been fired. The following week, Gerry DiNardo was introduced as the new head coach of the Commodores.

---

## In Hines' Sight

Football coaches, at all levels, are fired every year. I know the feeling—I have been fired. Your emotions take you on a butt-kicking ride. You feel like a criminal. You feel unclean and unwanted. Then you have yourself one fine pity party. Well, guess what? When the party's finally over . . . you're still fired.

It happens to the best of us. Heck, it could happen more than once. After you get up off the floor . . . where you fell after beating yourself up, it's time for a personal encounter with no one else but you.

I learned first hand that this one-on-one with yourself should be one of the most intimate, self-cleansing sessions you will ever have. No pretending. No covering up. No lying. No blaming. Just the absolute truth about yourself. Time to take total responsibility and fix whatever was wrong. Time to make promises to yourself that you know you will keep. And time to get up off your butt and move forward with the attitude that you are worthy to make happen, and receive, all the good that's coming your way. And believe it.

I have reported on numerous firings in my career, and I've known many in my industry who have been terminated. But I would venture to say that in almost every case it turned out to be the best thing that ever happened to the person. He or she either advanced to a better stage in a career or changed careers for the better. There is only one totally unacceptable option if you are ever fired. You do not quit.

❖ Now Hear This

Author and business leader Harvey Mackay tells the story about the high school basketball coach who was attempting to motivate his players to persevere through a difficult season. At the midpoint of the season he stood before the team and said, "Did Michael Jordan ever quit?"

The team responded, "No!"

He yelled. "What about the Wright brothers? Did they ever quit?"

Again the team yelled, "No!"

"Did Muhammad Ali ever quit?"

Again the team yelled, "No!"

"Did Elmer McAllister ever quit?"

There was a long silence. Finally one player was bold enough to ask, "Coach, who's Elmer McAllister? We never heard of him."

The coach snapped back, "Of course you never heard of him . . . he quit!"

### ❖ A Major(s) Tennessee Blunder

His name is John Terrill Majors, but many Vol fans think the *T* should stand for Tennessee. The legendary Johnny Majors was an All-American tailback for Tennessee and came home to coach the Vols in 1977 after winning a national championship at the University of Pittsburgh.

Speak with anyone who has ever known Johnny for any period of time, and they will likely have a great Johnny Majors story or two, or even three.

Gary Lundy, writing for the *Knoxville News-Sentinel*, reported that ESPN commentator Beano Cook, a former Pitt sports information director, says Majors remains "the most beloved Southerner of all time in Pennsylvania."

Former Michigan State coach Duffy Daugherty once introduced Johnny as "the only coach in the country with a father named Shirley and a mother named John." John's mother was Elizabeth, but her full name was John Elizabeth Bobo Majors.

I know John Majors as one of the most unforgettable characters of my career, and I too have several Johnny Majors stories.

The first time I met coach Majors was in 1976 in San Diego. He was in town to speak to some group and was wearing the most godawful, not just loud, but screaming loud, plaid sports coat I had ever seen. I interviewed him and we hit it off like two old friends, probably because of our Tennessee connections. He was funny and gave interesting answers, which we TV folks love.

The next time I laid eyes on Johnny was in the fall of 1983 at his weekly press briefing in Knoxville. I asked a question that day, and before he answered he looked at me for the longest moment then said, "Where do I know you from?" I reminded him of our meeting in San Diego seven years before, and he jokingly said I was welcome as long everything I said and reported about the football team was positive. When his press conference was over he invited me to have lunch with him in the cafeteria. From that day forward, my relationship with John Majors was, and remains, special.

Johnny loves to tell folks that I had the ability to make him say things he didn't want to say or things he didn't even know he was going to say. I believe it was the personal respect we had for each other. Johnny loved the fact that I always asked challenging but fair questions. Sometimes they were off-the-wall questions, which prompted Majors to ask me before we did interviews, "Okay, what dumb-ass question you gonna ask me today?"

At home games in Knoxville, after Johnny shook hands with the opposing coach, he knew I would soon find him for a quick interview as he walked off the field. Win or lose, I would get his first comments about the outcome as he walked to the locker room.

John had the reputation of being hard on his players and harder on his assistant coaches. I also know he was hard on himself. He has a delightful sense of humor and nobody, and I mean nobody, loves to tell a story more than John Majors.

I was on the board of a charity golf tournament in Nashville in the '80s. John was my guest each year, and often he would invite coaching buddies and friends to play as well. Over the years we have continued to play golf, and John Majors continues to be as competitive on the golf course as he ever was on the football field.

### ❖ Bumping and Grinding on Bourbon Street

I am often asked to name the most exciting game I ever saw. There are two: the Music City Miracle and the 1986 Sugar Bowl. I'll talk more about the MC Miracle in another chapter.

On January 1, 1986, the second-ranked Miami Hurricanes, coached by Jimmy Johnson, and number-eight Tennessee, under

Johnny Majors, met at the Super Dome. The atmosphere was electric. The 'Canes were favored and appeared dominant on the opening drive, as Miami scored on an eighteen-yard pass from Vinny Testaverde to Michael Irvin. Then the Tennessee defense took control, shutting down Miami's heralded passing attack, and the Vols went on to a shocking 35–7 victory in front of a Tennessee crowd that was out of their minds all night.

There's one more thing I need to tell you about from that Sugar Bowl trip: New Year's eve on Bourbon Street. We were scheduled to do a live shot at ten o'clock that night and had parked our truck on Bourbon Street, below the balcony of the hotel we would be broadcasting from. The street was so crowded that if anyone had fallen down it would've been days before they were found. Just as I began my live shot, I stepped to the side so our camera could pan the mostly drunken crowd below. Suddenly, a half-naked, fully inebriated woman appeared on top of our truck and began to remove the few pieces of clothing she had left. Of course, the crowd went wild. I immediately told our audience back in Nashville that this woman was most definitely not a part of our New Year's Eve broadcast plans, but I reasoned, "She was . . . a bonus." Our camera quickly panned away from her, before she became totally X-rated. With nothing on but lipstick, she began to "bump and grind" on a certain part of our satellite equipment. By now the crowd was at riot stage, and the cops were frantically trying to get her off the truck, when all of a sudden she dove into the crowd, never to be seen again.

I must tell you, it was one of my finest moments of concentration, as I continued to talk about the Tennessee-Miami game (at that point who cared, right?) while giving updates on the naked woman below, until she finally disappeared into the sea of orange and white behind me. That, by the way, is the only pornographic videotape that exists in the NewsChannel 5 archives today . . . that I know of.

I should have entered that live shot from Bourbon Street for an Emmy award under the category of best sports comedy.

### ❖ Nashville Fairgrounds Speedway—The Real Story

I arrived back in Nashville in the early 1980s, just in time to witness one of the city's greatest misfortunes. Nashville Fairgrounds

Speedway was one of the crown jewels of sports and entertainment in those days. Saturday night racing at the Fairgrounds, where the future stars of Nascar trained, drew capacity crowds, and the speedway showcased two Winston Cup dates each year.

All that changed in 1984, however, when Nascar forever pulled the two Cup dates the speedway had held since 1958. The track was never the same again. Here, for the first time, is the story of what really happened and why.

Gary Baker, a prominent Nashville attorney (Baker, Campbell & Parsons) who owned several businesses and various real estate investments, had a dream. He wanted to build a "superspeedway" in middle Tennessee, and he was well on his way.

Baker already owned Bristol Motor Speedway, had a minority interest in Atlanta Motor Speedway, and was the lease-holder for the Fairgrounds Speedway. A new track would take lots of money and Baker, looking for financing, began holding talks with Opryland (or NLT, the holding company for Opryland) about investing in the project. Baker had purchased hundreds of acres of land where Cool Springs Galleria is now for the proposed site. Hoping to cover all his bases, he took a contingent of Franklin city officials to a race in Charlotte to help sell them on his plan.

That's when Gary got a phone call from Ralph Seagraves of R. J. Reynolds Tobacco company, sponsor of the Winston Cup series. Ralph told Baker to expect a call from Warner Hodgdon. Hodgdon was a California businessman who owned or had a major interest in six racetracks around the country and also owned a 50 percent interest in Junior Johnson racing.

Baker met Hodgdon in Nashville a short time later, and they formed a partnership. In the deal, Baker sold Hodgdon 50 percent of the Bristol and Nashville speedways, and their agreement included a put-call clause (buy-sell) if either ever wanted to exercise it.

It wasn't long before Baker and Hodgdon had a major disagreement. Hodgdon thought they should expand the Fairgrounds Speedway, much like the track at Richmond, instead of building on Baker's land. They argued for a year.

In 1983, Baker began to panic because the lease and the two Winston Cup dates for the Fairgrounds Speedway would run out in 1987. Nascar wanted the new track in place for the '87 season, and Baker knew it would take years to finance and build. Time was running out. Baker was tired of trying to convince Hodgdon to build a new track and initiated the put-call agreement, fully expecting Hodgdon to sell. According to the clause, the one who wanted to buy would set the price, and the partner could either accept or reject the offer. If he refused to sell, he then was obligated to buy at the price his partner had set.

"My pride will not allow me to sell to you," Hodgdon told Baker, and that was it. Baker had to sell his interest in both speedways: Bristol and the Fairgrounds. Hodgdon now had them both, and Baker was out. He was devastated. He had rolled the dice in the biggest gamble of his life and lost.

Hodgdon's national operation of tracks and other business ventures would last one more year. In January of 1985, he filed for bankruptcy, facing lawsuits totaling over 50 million dollars. His empire had crumbled, and Nashville would forever feel the pain of that colossal collapse. As soon as Hodgdon filed for bankruptcy, Nascar pulled their two Winston Cup dates from the Fairgrounds Speedway, never to return.

As soon as Hodgdon filed for bankruptcy, Gary Baker immediately picked up the pieces. He bought back the final three years of the original speedway lease he held with Hodgdon, and racing continued on Saturday nights, with sellout crowds. But the damage had been done. Nascar had soured on the speedway, and the track was suddenly bad news, forever ending Cup racing in Music City.

Down but not out, Baker regrouped. He came up with his most ambitious, if not implausible, scheme yet. He would buy . . . Nascar, and he had an ally. As if he hadn't learned enough from his previous partnership with Warner Hodgdon, he teamed up with George Gillett Jr.

Like Baker, Gillett was a high-stakes gambler. Gillett was also a former 20 percent owner of the Miami Dolphins. He had purchased the almost defunct Harlem Globetrotters and re-energized them with an ambitious marketing campaign. Gillett also owned a stable of TV stations, including WSM-TV in Nashville, which he changed to WSMV-TV in the early '80s. This was the time to strike. Baker and Gillett were prepared and ready to make an offer to buy Nascar.

After some discussion, it was agreed that only Baker would go to Daytona to talk with Bill France Jr. and roll out their plan for purchase.

Baker met with France and current Nascar president Mike Helton for an hour. Baker then said he wanted to meet privately with France, and Helton was excused from the meeting. Baker and France would talk for another two hours. At one point France was being hypothetical, telling Baker if he could turn the clock back and start Nascar all over, Nashville would be his choice for the first track built after Daytona. That's how much value he placed on the Nashville market.

Their meeting ended with France telling Baker it had been an interesting three hours and he wanted to think about everything that had been said. He told Baker there would be one more conversation relative to their meeting.

Several weeks later, Baker received his answer when France called to say he had thought seriously about the offer but had decided not to sell. Baker still held the Speedway lease, but France was not comfortable with the city politics and the stability of the track. He told Baker he was sorry, but the two Winston Cup dates would be moved elsewhere.

The really sad component of this story is that Nashville's economy has been the big loser, and it could have been avoided. The business of the Speedway was made too complex, and it was badly mismanaged by the Fairboard. If there had been cordial cooperation between the governing body and its lease holders for the past three decades, Cup racing in Nashville could have been salvaged. Hundreds of millions of dollars lost is surely enough to make mayors and city council members run for the wailing walls.

## In Hines' Sight

I have never known an entrepreneur who was afraid of failure. They view failure differently than the average person does. To them failure is an irritant, something to brush aside and forget. They see things the rest of us don't. They do things we think are nuts. Their need to win is so great that they spend no time wallowing in regret. They are quick to move on to the next thing, which they are certain will reward them with victory.

All our lives are filled with defining moments—a handshake that becomes a friend for life, an encouraging word to someone ready to let go, the completion of a project long in its journey, the beginning of something new, and the realization that success leaves clues but so does failure. We are only defeated . . . if we say we are.

> If we will . . .
> Risk more than others think is safe
> Care more than others think is wise
> Dream more than others think is practical
> Expect more than others think is possible
> There is nothing in this world we cannot accomplish.
> —Claude Thomas Bissell

### ❖ Doing Twenty Years with Mark

"Let's bring in NewsChannel 5's Mark Howard."

I must have uttered that phrase on the air several thousand times in my twenty-year association with Mark Howard, the master of quips and the "au fait" of sports. Mark came to work for Channel 5 in 1986 as our weekend sports anchor and weekday reporter, and my life was never the same again.

Mark and I were different in some ways, yet we were alike in so many other ways. Mark is a walking, talking sports encyclopedia, and I remain constantly amazed at the depth of his knowledge. He ignites everyone around him with his fervor and passion. Mark has an amazing ability to analyze and communicate his thoughts and feelings about any subject, from politics, to religion, to pop culture. He has never straddled the fence on any controversy, and he always has an opinion. If yours doesn't agree with his, you better be ready for some spicy dialog.

In the early years, most people who wanted a career in broadcasting got into radio first before embarking on a television career. Mark did radio first, then TV, and he is now arguably Nashville's top radio sports talk-show host. Mark's enthusiasm and expertise on everything sports enables him to stand out in a crowded field.

As a skilled craftsman with words, Mark mastered both TV and radio with equal thunder. Before computers, when I needed to know something, I just googled Mark's brain.

We did not always agree, and we certainly had our differences over the years. But the great thing about my friendship with Mark was that we always had each others' backs. Still do. There is nothing I wouldn't do for him. He's the best.

## ❖ Hey Frank . . . It Was Mark's Fault

Just before he signed his last contract, there were rumors that Titans all-pro tight end Frank Wycheck might be traded. Naturally, this was a hot story, and we wanted Wycheck to comment on it. He was hosting a charity motorcycle ride on a Sunday afternoon, and Mark Howard, who at that time anchored the weekend sports, sent photographer Bob Kusek to interview him about the trade rumors. Bob's first question to Wycheck was about the ride, then Bob asked him to comment on the possibility of him being traded. Wycheck did not appreciate the question, believing Bob had blindsided him. He became upset. Kusek, of course, was only doing what Mark had asked him to do. Wycheck let it be known in no uncertain terms that he was not at all happy with Kusek's question. Because of that incident, Wycheck held a grudge against all of us at NewsChannel 5 for several years. Just a few years later, however, Wycheck would become a teammate of Howard's each morning on the Wake Up Zone on 104.5. Now, as a veteran of talk radio, Wycheck understands what it means to be a pro on the other side of the mike, and he has leaned to ask the tough, uncomfortable questions when needed.

## ❖ The Sounds of Baseball

Larry Schmittou had it figured out before he ever brought minor league baseball to Nashville in 1978. He would earn profits not from ticket sales but from the sale of souvenirs and concessions. His team of investors, which included country music entertainers Conway Twitty, Larry Gatlin, Jerry Reed, Richard Sterban of the Oak Ridge Boys, and Cal Smith, believed in his business philosophy as well. And because it worked, the Middle Tennessee sports landscape improved dramatically.

I have known Larry Schmittou since 1971 when he was the baseball coach at Vanderbilt. He coached and recruited using the same intangible that made him an ultra-successful minor league team owner: passion for the game.

Larry's exterior can be a bit rough and gruff for some people, and he never had a problem calling out members of the media when he thought his team was not getting its fair share of publicity.

He would call me at the station on occasion and say something like, "I just watched your ten o'clock sportscast. You showed highlights from the Braves . . . losing, first-round highlights from some golf tournament that probably not too many people care about, and a sound bite about an upcoming car race. Were you aware the Sounds played at home tonight?" Then he would sarcastically add, "I guess I'm going to have to invest in a camera to shoot the game and bring you the highlights."

It became a running joke between us, and every time I saw Larry after that I would ask, "You bought that camera yet, Larry?"

When you mortgage your home to help pay for the franchise, you have a right to be assertive and pushy on its behalf. Lucky for him, Larry had no problem in that area, nor did he hesitate to ask for help with things he knew nothing about. For example, he called on Ray Danner, founder of Shoney's, to teach him about food for concessions.

Larry was a huge believer in promoting his product, and he understood that minor league baseball was more than anything else a family affair. Just about any night you went to Greer Stadium, you would enjoy such promotions as Tight Fittin' Jeans night, the San Diego Chicken, or the Beach Boys in concert. Schmittou was one of the first minor league team owners to have faith night at the stadium. He got a call one day from an atheist who told Larry he was going to sue him. Schmittou's response, "Sue me, please! I need the publicity." The old boy definitely has a sense of humor. The Sounds were highly successful under Schmittou's ownership for nineteen years. Then in 1997, he sold the team. Why, after fulfilling his dream to bring minor league baseball to Nashville and after so many years of success?

"The Titans drove me out," Schmittou told me. He said he saw the writing on the wall and knew there were only so many dollars available for people to spend on entertainment, and the Titans (then the Oilers) would be that twelve-thousand-pound elephant, and he wanted to get out while he could.

When Larry sold the Sounds, he partnered with Rick Scott, an executive with Hospital Corporation of America (now the governor of Florida), and they looked at buying the Kansas City Royals, but it didn't work out.

Looking for something to do, Schmittou bought his first bowling alley in 2000, and now, under the name Strike and Spare Family Fun Centers, he owns the third largest chain in the nation.

So where did a former Vanderbilt baseball coach get such a competitive spirit for entrepreneurship? "It was born out of need," he said, and he told me this story. One year, Vanderbilt was invited to play in a baseball tournament in Hawaii, but on his budget of twelve thousand dollars there was no way that would happen. So he came up with the idea to rent a 747 and sell seats for a week's vacation to Hawaii. He sold 445 seats. His team and more than 400 of their closest friends enjoyed a week in paradise, and "Nashville Sports Tours" was born.

## In Hines' Sight

Every successful person I have observed in my forty-plus years of sports broadcasting has worn that same invisible badge over their heart that says: "I believe." It is the one essential for success. Many times these people were not the most talented or gifted person at what they did, but they believed in themselves with a vision only they could see. Then they practiced harder and outworked everybody else.

As Napoleon Hill, best-selling author of *Think and Grow Rich,* said, "What the mind of man can conceive and believe, it can achieve."

*There are only three real sports: bull-fighting, car racing and mountain climbing. All the others are mere games.*

ERNEST HEMINGWAY

# Music City
# Duffers and Drivers

NASHVILLE • 1988–1995

❖ A Golf Tournament That Cooked

In 1988, the first annual LPGA Sara Lee Golf Classic was held at the Hermitage Golf Course in Old Hickory, Tennessee. It quickly became a Middle Tennessee institution that fans, volunteers, and the media alike looked forward to each year.

It was arguably the best organized and executed sporting event in the area for the next eleven years, due to the first-class style and leadership of Clyde Russell, Bill Cecil, Mike Eller, Ray Danner, Tina Myers, and Billie Romine, who made the tournament a joy for all who attended.

I will always be in awe of the one thousand-plus volunteers, many of whom took their vacations each summer to work the tournament. For them it truly was a labor of love. But the one thing that really made this event special were the players. As a group they were always cordial and appreciative (not all athletes are) of the coverage they received from the media.

Nancy Lopez was the favorite of both the fans and the media. She gladly assumed the role of LPGA ambassador. She loved promoting the game, its traditions, and its values, and she loved coming to Nashville each year because of the wonderful bond she developed with its legions of fans. She was never more adored than when she won the 1991 Sara Lee while pregnant with her third child.

Nancy was a guest of mine on several occasions on *Sportsline* on NewsChannel 5 Plus, the hour-long talk show I hosted, and her appearances always drew big numbers.

None of us who covered the Sara Lee will ever forget, and we will forever be touched by, our association with Heather Farr. The attractive twenty-four-year-old player from Phoenix was diagnosed with breast cancer in 1989, and her battle with the disease was chronicled by the national media for the next four years. She died in 1993 at age twenty-eight. A memorial marker for Heather can be seen just behind the pro shop and in front of the eighteenth green at the Hermitage Golf Course.

### ❖ Golf's Singing Ambassador

You will look far and wide before finding a superstar as charming and unassuming as Vincent Grant Gill. Vince, a Music City icon and international ambassador for Nashville, lent his name and talents to the Sara Lee Golf Classic, hosting the Vince Gill Celebrity Skins Game each year. When the tournament moved to the Legends Club of Tennessee in Franklin in 2000 as the Electrolux USA Championship, Vince and his wife, Amy Grant, were the hosts. There is no debate that the LPGA's presence in Middle Tennessee would not have been as successful or fun without Vince Gill's involvement. Since 1993, Vince has hosted the Vinny Pro-Celebrity at the Golf Club of Tennessee, with the proceeds going to Junior golf in Tennessee.

### ❖ A Seven-Year Phantasmagoria

The day I returned from covering Tennessee in the 1989 Cotton Bowl in Dallas (the Vols beat Arkansas 31–27), I went to my mailbox and found a registered letter from an attorney in Clarksville. I was being sued for several hundred thousand dollars. For the next seven years, Pat and I lived as if we were stuck in an elevator. We had been in the process of looking for property to build a house, but with this hanging over our heads, not knowing whether or not we were facing financial ruin, our lives were on hold.

Thorold Ramsey was my partner in a venture to buy a radio

station in Clarksville. Thorold already owned a station in McMinnville, and we put up earnest money for the purchase of WJZM. As we understood it, our agreement stipulated that if we backed out of the deal, the owners of the station, Charlie Malone and John Bailey, would keep the earnest money, and we would walk away from the sale. One month before the papers were to be signed, Thorold and I agreed to back out of the buy because of certain financial information we were not getting from the owners. I called Charlie Malone and told him we had decided not to go through with the purchase. I said I understood that they would keep the earnest money as a result. Malone and Bailey decided to sue us instead.

Thorold and I hired the Nashville firm of Neal and Harwell to represent us, but after several years we had to switch to a law firm in Clarksville, because our case would be tried there. We hired the firm of Rassas & Rassas, which meant Mark Rassas would have to get up to speed on our case, which took several more years. Finally, after seven long years, with the attorney meter always running, our case went to court. We thought it would be decided in several days. At noon on Friday the fifth day, the jury got the case and began their deliberations. Pat and I stayed in a motel in Clarksville most of that week, and of course I had not been on the air at all. That Thursday night we turned out the lights about midnight, and I got down on my knees by the bed. I prayed as honestly as I knew how, telling the Lord that if Thorold and I had actually caused the station owners real damage, as they said we had—to the tune of a half million dollars—then let the verdict be guilty, and I would leave it up to Him (God) as to how we would pay the damages. But if we were not guilty, let the verdict reflect that as well. Late Friday afternoon, the jury returned with their verdict: not guilty. Our joy and exhilaration were indescribable. We had our lives back, and I said a silent prayer of thanks. Then I couldn't wait to get out of Dodge.

## In Hines' Sight

As a result of that seven-year ordeal, I learned one of the greatest lessons of my life. Never, ever sign your name to anything of importance, in any business transaction, without a good attorney by your side each and every step . . . in the end, whatever you have to pay them is worth it.

### ❖ Going Around in Circles at Daytona

Don't let anybody tell you any different. It's about gas fumes, the smell of rubber, asphalt sun-tans, pit-lizards (young women in skimpy clothing), and the sights and sounds of cars traveling at over two hundred miles per hour that draw millions each year to the sport of car racing. I must admit I am attracted to all that . . . most of it anyway.

I had been going to Daytona for most of the 1980s to cover the 500, but 1989 would turn out to be a very special year for several reasons, the first of which was we were all going to be movie stars. During the twin qualifying races for the 500, they were filming a scene from the movie *Days of Thunder*, staring Tom Cruise and Nicole Kidman. The focus of the scene was a crash in the infield on the front straightaway. A helicopter was landing to evacuate the injured driver. I told photographer Al T. Cobb to climb on the roof of pit road for a better shot of the scene. Huge mistake. Just as Al was in position to start shooting, a security guard blew his whistle, signaling for Al to come down off the roof. When Al climbed down, the guard took his credential, telling him he would have to leave the track. Knowing we were in big trouble and realizing it was my fault, I walked over to the guard and implored him to give us a break. Nothing doing. He said Al would have to leave the track, and the only way he would get back in was to talk with the officials at the media center.

Talk about a feeling of despair. We were completely at the mercy of Nascar. You bet I walked into that meeting with my hands in my pockets as meek and humble as I have ever been. I begged, and I pleaded. I explained that I would lose my job if Al couldn't go back and cover the race. It was a performance worthy of an Academy Award. I was brilliant in remorse, and a huge disaster was avoided.

Now for some *Days of Thunder* trivia. Additional footage of the movie was shot during the 1990 Daytona 500, with the late Bobby Hamilton of Nashville driving one of two cars added to the rear of the field for the purpose of shooting them for the film. Hamilton reportedly was paid fifteen thousand dollars by Rick Hendrick to drive the camera car. At the time, Bobby was making about 185 dollars a week driving a wrecker. He drove so well Hendrick hired him for the next Nascar race in Phoenix and for the remainder of the season.

### ❖ Running on Fumes

Racing, like all sports, really, is all about numbers. The '89 Daytona 500 would be Darrell Waltrip's 17th try to win the Super Bowl of Nascar, and he was driving the number 17 Tide Chevrolet. Al and I were camped in Waltrip's pit with about 50 laps remaining in the 500 to capture his final pit stop. A caution came out with 40 laps to go, and Jeff Hammond, Waltrip's crew chief, told him to stay out and not pit. Al had the camera microphone wired into Waltrip's radio communication, and recorded Darrell's response. "Do we have enough gas? Can we go all the way?"

Hammond hesitated, then said, "It will be close."

One by one the race leaders began to pit for fuel. Waltrip was now second, trailing only Alan Kulwicki. Suddenly, Kulwicki had a flat tire on lap 196, and Waltrip took the lead.

Would there be enough gas to make it? With two laps to go, the fuel pressure gauge dropped to zero. Not once, but twice. Then suddenly the fuel gauge came back up. Waltrip came out of turn four with a six-second lead on Ken Schrader, and he held his breath to the finish line to win the Daytona 500 . . . and his car ran out of gas on his way to victory lane. There were tears of joy on the faces of Waltrip's crew members as the wild celebration got underway.

As Al and I made our way to victory circle, we encountered Darrell's wife, Stevie, on the way. Tears were streaming down her face. With our camera rolling, all Stevie could say was, "I am so happy for Darrell. He has worked so hard for this day."

Darrell climbed out of his car, the happiest champion I had ever seen. He shouted to CBS pit reporter Mike Joy, "I won the Daytona 500. I won the Daytona 500! Wait, this is the Daytona 500, ain't it? Thank God!" Waltrip then performed the "Ickey Shuffle" in victory lane, spiking his helmet to the concrete.

It took Darrell Waltrip seventeen years to win the biggest race in Nascar. Success really is all about climbing mountains . . . one after another. The only way to reach the summit is to climb. If there is another way, please let me know.

Let us never forget the climb. No matter the size of the prize. Every painful, heartbreaking step. Sometimes we fall. But we get back up. Sometimes we quit. But we start again, and always our resilience amazes us. With the pinnacle of our efforts in sight, our breathing becomes heavier, our smile grows wider, tears wash our face, and suddenly we are there. Then . . . joy, jubilation, euphoria. Remember, it's all about the climb. Said professional curmudgeon Andy Rooney: "Have fun while you are climbing. I've learned that everyone wants to live on top of the mountain, but all the happiness and growth occurs while you're climbing it."

## ❖ A Video Tribute

In late 1989, photographer Al T. Cobb stuck his head in my office one day and said, "Hope, why don't we produce a video of Darrell Waltrip's career?" And I said, "And we could sell it to ESPN or market it ourselves. Yeah, let's do it."

Al and I spent the next few weeks mapping out a strategy for our video, which would include following Darrell to several races with total access to him and his crew. I proposed the idea to DW, and he liked it. Darrell agreed to pay for the cost of production, and then we would split the profits 50-50. I received permission from my bosses at Channel 5, and we began production in 1990 at the Daytona 500.

A few weeks later, we flew with Darrell on his plane to Talladega for testing. Dale Earnhardt was also there that day. One of the best features of the video was a conversation between Waltrip and Earnhardt as they discussed testing together on the track and agreed on rules for racing against each other. Dale was in a playful mood that day and enjoyed taking shots at Darrell and his driving ability.

We spent most of 1990 traveling to races, as I interviewed drivers, crew members, Nascar officials, and others who knew Darrell and had stories to tell about his illustrious career. I contracted with the Gatlin Brothers music publishing company to write and produce music for the video. When it was completed, we had produced almost an hour. I called ESPN, and they were interested in airing the video, but they wanted an exclusive contract, which meant we wouldn't be able to market it to the public. We decided against ESPN and marketed it nationally through Darrell's fan club. It was one of the best pieces of work I had ever been involved in, and Darrell was equally proud of the finished product.

## ❖ Hope Productions

With the completion of the Darrell Waltrip video and sales going quite well, my entrepreneurial spirit was born. I came up with the idea of selling advertising on the side of eighteen-wheelers. I stole the idea from Nascar, of course. Racecars are traveling billboards. Why not eighteen-wheelers? I talked my best friend from college Chuck Cooper into joining me, and we formed an advertising business called Truck Ad and a production company called Hope Productions. I talked it over with Channel 5 station manager Lem Lewis, and he gave me his okay, as long as it didn't interfere with my work for the station. With Truck Ads, we sold advertising on eighteen-wheelers that traveled throughout the Southeast. Our first customer was Opryland and the Grand Ole Opry. With Hope Productions, we produced corporate marketing videos for customers in middle Tennessee. I had already been producing a marketing video for the Sara Lee Golf Classic each year, and it made sense to do the same for other companies. Well, guess what? After a year of burning the candle at both ends, I had to make a decision. Doing both jobs was killing me. Do I leave Channel 5 and become a full-time entrepreneur or suspend business operations? I chose to continue my TV career, and thus Truck Ad and Hope Productions ceased to exist. I had a great time with those two companies, and I learned so much about doing business, but I wasn't ready to leave TV, and no way could I continue to do both. I made the right decision, at the right time.

### ❖ Handcuffed in Atlanta

After covering the 1991 World Series in Atlanta, between the Braves and the Minnesota Twins, I came away with many lasting memories. I spent some time with my good friend Lewis Grizzard (whom I've already written about) and visited with Hall of Famer Johnny Bench. I had my picture taken with Johnny and my son Lyman during batting practice. I saw Ted Turner and Jane Fonda and President Jimmy Carter. I talked with Deion Sanders and Hank Aaron. But it is what happened in the parking lot of Atlanta-Fulton County Stadium before game three that scared the absolute hell out of me.

Channel 5 photographer Mike Radford and I had just purchased some World Series memorabilia, and we were back at our car in the parking lot, placing the items in the trunk. Since I was carrying our expense money, I reached into my pocket and pulled out a wad of cash, handing Mike several bills for his game expenses. The trunk lid was open as we stood there exchanging money. Suddenly, we heard, "Hold it right there. Atlanta police! Do not move."

A very cold chill ran down my spine as I turned to see two fast-approaching undercover police officers flashing their badges with one hand, a firm grip on their gun holsters with the other. I about had a heart attack. Before I knew what was happening, they grabbed Mike and me and spun us around, placing our hands behind our backs. That's when I felt cold steel wrapping around my wrists.

"Officers, wait a minute, please. What's this all about?" I pleaded.

"We've been watching you the past few minutes," one of them said. "What's in the bag in the trunk?"

"Just some items we just bought to take home."

By now one of the officers had the sack and dumped the contents out. There were several World Series T-shirts, caps, and other items. "We saw you hand him some money. Where's the dope?"

I had seen this scene a dozen times in movies, but my God, this time it was happening to me. "Officer, I swear. There is no dope. You've got to believe me. We're here to cover the series for a TV station in Nashville. Look at our media passes hanging around our necks." By now I was sweating bullets. The officers thoroughly searched the trunk and inside of our car as well as our clothes. Of course, they found nothing.

"Okay, looks like you're who you say you are. Sorry, we made a mistake," one of them said, taking the handcuffs off, sounding as if he really hated to apologize. "When we saw you exchange money, with the trunk of the car open, we assumed you were dealing drugs. That was a bad move. Lots of drug deals going down here in the parking lot. Again, we apologize. Hope you understand. Enjoy the game." They left Mike and me standing there with the trunk still open. We looked at each other, still in shock, not saying a word as Mike slammed the trunk lid. "Well, Mike," I said as we headed toward the stadium, "Let's see if the World Series can top that for excitement."

## ❖ Ugly Departure in Knoxville

It was November. Friday the 13th, 1992. Johnny Majors had been forced to resign during that week and would address the media in Memphis the day before the Vols faced Memphis State. My photographer and I hopped on a small twin-engine plane and flew to Memphis for the press conference. Majors took no questions following his comments and walked out of the press gathering with his wife, Mary Lynn.

Twenty years later, in March 2012, I met Coach Majors for breakfast at the Nashville Airport Marriott, and for two hours we talked about the past and a lot about the present.

The seventy-seven-year-old Majors told me he was having too much fun with his life to spend any time thinking about his ignominious demise, as he calls it. Majors left Tennessee as a result of a bitter betrayal by four men whom he has yet to forgive. The men were Phillip Fulmer, who replaced Majors as head coach; athletics director Doug Dickey; UT Athletics Board member Bill Johnson; and university president Joe Johnson. Those wounds may never heal, but Majors has re-established a relationship with the university and attends football practice and games on a regular basis.

Majors currently owns a company that produces Nike Coach

of the Year Clinics across the country. He is busy most weekends traveling to the clinics.

I asked the coach if he had been keeping up with the stories of the New Orleans Saints big-money bounty payments for knocking certain opponents out of games . . . and if that sort of thing ever happened on the college level.

He said he never heard of anything like that happening anytime he was coaching, but he was certainly familiar with so-called incentive money for players who accomplished good things during a game. "In fact," he said with a wink, "I received several ten-dollar handshakes when I played."

## ❖ Eddie Fogler Was Not a Fan

Former Vanderbilt men's basketball coach Eddie Fogler was not a fan of mine. Not after a certain incident at the Hermitage Golf Course in the early 1990s. Eddie had been playing golf about a year and wasn't very good. I was shooting a Channel 5 sports promo on the par-3 fifth hole, which is across water, when Eddie and his playing partner showed up to tee off. I instructed my photographer to shoot Eddie's tee shot and to follow the ball.

It was an ugly duck hook that slammed into the water.

That evening during the six o'clock news, I explained that Fogler had recently taken up golf, then I showed his snap hook off the tee. I then said, jokingly, "Looks like Eddie needs a few more lessons before he's ready for prime time."

Little did I realize Fogler's reaction would result in bitter agitation and anger. I thought I was giving viewers a glimpse of his human side. Not so, according to Eddie. Actually Eddie didn't tell me how peeved he was. He told Mark Howard, who was doing a preseason interview with him. Mark came back and said he couldn't believe how upset Fogler was. Mark said Eddie was making derogatory remarks about me to his friends and associates. To which I replied, "Tell Eddie I hope his verbal shots are a lot better than his golf shots," and I laughed the whole thing off.

But Eddie wouldn't let it go. Every time he saw Mark, he would say something snide about me. "Why doesn't Eddie call me if he has a problem?" I said to Mark, who shrugged his shoulders and said, "Leave me out of this."

I was tired of hearing him belly-ache about something so inane, so I picked up the phone and called Eddie for a meeting, which he agreed to in his office. The day of our meeting, he made me wait about thirty minutes. Okay, I got it. It was his way of saying, When you are on my turf we play by my rules. Eddie always had strict rules in dealing with the media. He certainly didn't go out of his way to be friendly, and he was never accused of being "Mister Happy." So I knew what I was dealing with.

Finally he showed up for our meeting and seated himself behind his desk without a greeting. He said, "If you had been in a bar with a camera, and I was in there drinking a beer . . . would you put that on TV?" He leaned across his desk.

"Only if you were drunk," I responded with a chuckle. "No, Eddie, I would not put that on TV. Are you trying to equate that with your golf shot?"

"I'm just trying to figure you out," he said, not smiling.

"Well, I'm no mystery, I can assure you. I did it because people love seeing public figures in unfamiliar situations, and honestly I thought you were big enough to laugh about it. Tell you what. I'll show it again and tell everyone how sorry I am for showing it, because you couldn't handle it . . . I'm kidding, Eddie! Why don't we just agree to disagree, shake hands, and get on with the rest of our lives." We both stood up and shook hands. Meeting over. As I walked to the door, I turned and said, "Hey, Eddie, I'll buy you a beer tonight, after the early news. No cameras . . . I promise."

## ❖ The Lady of Gold

The Italians nicknamed her *La Gazzella Negra* ("The Black Gazelle"); to the French she was *La Perle Noire* ("The Black Pearl"). To her family and friends she was simply . . . Wilma. But there was nothing simple about Wilma Rudolph, the former Tennessee State University Tigerbelle who became the first American woman to win three gold medals in track and field at the 1960 Olympics in Rome. The road to gold for the Clarksville, Tennessee, native, however, was anything but easy. Wilma was born premature and contracted polio at age four. She lost the use of her left leg and had to wear a brace and walk with crutches, but with physical therapy she overcame those disabilities.

Over the years I had become friends with Wilma, and like everybody else I was devastated when she was diagnosed with a malignant brain tumor. She died November 12, 1994.

Vickie Yates and I hosted a show on Channel 5 devoted to the life of Wilma Rudolph. The program ended with a tribute I wrote in her honor. I was privileged to be asked to read it at her funeral in Clarksville.

### The Lady of Gold
### A Biography in Motion

*From clay in the Potter's hand was molded something magnificent, and it would become the standard by which others would measure and be measured.*

*She was a child with an affliction, but already growing within was an equalizer, the seed of greatness.*

*And out of that adversity, as others moaned she would never recover, burst forth a desire and resolve of mind and character that would enable her to achieve her position among the athletic nobility of the ages.*

*Her legs were named Brilliance and Splendor, and they carried her to mountain tops only a few have ever experienced.*

*As the years passed and separated us from her athletic accomplishments, Wilma Rudolph's stature as a human being had grown to be equally admired.*

*She was a true citizen of the world.*

*Embraced by all cultures and elevated to royalty in many countries of Europe, I knew Wilma Rudolph, not only as an athlete, but as a "grand lady."*

*A proud woman, yet humble in spirit, generous in serving the needs of others, and with an absolute passion for life.*

*Yes, Wilma knew all about struggles and battles.*

*She lost a few, but won her share, and then some . . . and it's the spirit of her living we will remember.*

*Wilma Rudolph, I know, fulfilled her purpose here on earth. And what a splendid purpose it was.*

*And so, it remains for us to inspect, learn from, and apply what she left behind.*

*It's no magic formula, I can assure you.*

*All the great ones have it. . . . It's called heart, and with it you can soar like the eagles to any height you desire.*

*So let's all keep looking up, because the next lightning bolt from the sky just might be Wilma Rudolph with wings on her feet . . . off on another race with the wind.*

## In Hines' Sight

Why is it that those who have been burdened with handicaps often outperform others who have been blessed by nature? In fact we often see the more gifted athlete, the better educated, the wealthy pushed aside by someone nobody ever heard of, but whose determination and energy makes them a force to be reckoned with.

The conclusion must be because those favored with advantages look to material things for their success. They depend on wealth, family, friends, or abilities, and when those things fail, they crumble.

When a person has none of those advantages, he or she must look for success somewhere else. The turning point in the lives of most successful people usually comes during some moment of crisis. It was in that adversity that they looked deep inside themselves to find their seed of equivalent benefit.

## ❖ The Plus

NewsChannel 5 station manager Lem Lewis came up with a brilliant idea in the mid '90s. He contracted with a local cable company to program a channel that would be dedicated specifically for our use. Part of the programming was a one-hour live sports talk show Monday through Thursday each week.

I began hosting *Sportsline* on Channel 5 Plus in 1996 each evening from 8:00 to 9:00 p.m. My very first guest was Vanderbilt athletic director Todd Turner. The show afforded me the opportunity to do in-depth interviews with coaches and players on a daily basis that I would otherwise have never experienced.

In fifteen years hosting *Sportsline*, there were some unforgettable and, yes, some very forgettable characters that I interviewed. Boxing promoter Don King leads the list of off-the-wall characters. This man has no limits or boundaries where self-aggrandizement and promotion are concerned. But if I were promoting something, you better believe he is the man I would hire, if I could afford him.

Former LSU basketball coach Dale Brown was one of the most interesting and introspective people I ever interviewed. He is a master motivator and has a tremendous heart for the disadvantaged. Michael Franzese, the former New York mobster with the Colombo crime family who left the underworld and formed a foundation for helping youth, becoming a motivational speaker in the process, was perhaps the most fascinating interview I ever did. Sitting across from Lady Vols coach Pat Summitt, I was mesmerized, almost hypnotized, by her eyes.

I even did a live edition of *Sportsline* on the beach behind the Fontainebleau Hotel in Miami when the Vols played Nebraska in the Orange Bowl in 1998. My guests were David Climer, columnist for the *Tennessean*, and Pete Kutz, who was one of UT's top fundraisers, along with his wife, Carol. Pete later became a member of the University of Tennessee athletic board.

❖ Hope Hines 4Kids Golf Classic

In early 1997, Dr. Gerald Stowe, president of the Tennessee Baptist Children's Home in Franklin, asked me if I would help with a golf tournament they were putting on for the benefit of the children's home. I was only too glad to help, and I am proud to say I have been associated with that tournament every year since. It is now called the Hope Hines 4Kids Golf Classic, and we have raised over half a million dollars for abused and abandoned boys and girls of every faith, and no faith, who live on the Franklin campus. I am thankful to Vince Gill, Darrell Waltrip, and many, many other Middle Tennessee celebrities, including Titans and Predators as well as country music entertainers for their help and support over the past fifteen years. Of course, no charitable organization could exist without wonderful sponsors and players who sustain our tournament each year. Hats off to our board of directors, which simply makes it happen each year.

# Titans, Preds, and Beyond

### NASHVILLE 1995–2011

❖ Who's Coming to Town?

Sometime in June 1995, I was speaking to a noon civic organization, and someone in the audience asked the question, "Would Nashville ever be a candidate for an NFL franchise?"

I laughed out loud and said something like, "Are you kidding? No! Nashville would never get an NFL team. Memphis maybe. But never Nashville."

Six months later, on November 16 at 10:47 a.m., Mayor Phil Bredesen and Houston Oilers owner Bud Adams signed the agreement to bring the Oilers to Nashville, and with the stroke of a pen, Music City was forever changed.

I will never forget Bud Adams standing on the steps at the Metro Courthouse, surrounded by the state's power brokers and looking out over the crowd, which included the media and other interested onlookers. He shouted, "Are you ready for some football?" And the rest, as they say . . . is history.

❖ A Texas Size Meeting with Bud

Bud Adams has an office in Houston the size of a car dealer's showroom (and he needs it) filled with fifty-two years' worth of NFL stuff. During the spring of 1996, Adams welcomed members of the

Nashville media to his office, where we conducted one-on-one interviews with the man who, along with the late Lamar Hunt of the Kansas City Chiefs, founded the AFL in 1960. Bud, by the way, paid a whopping twenty-five thousand for the Oilers franchise—not a bad investment, considering the franchise is now valued at almost a billion dollars.

I interviewed Bud that day and found him engaging, interesting, and very enthusiastic about the Oilers' pending move to Nashville. All around his office is memorabilia from his days as an NFL owner and his Cherokee Indian heritage, which he is quite proud of. I was the last of the interviewers that day, and when the interview was over, he graciously showed me around his office, pointing out historical facts about certain items. He even showed me one of his storage rooms (he had several), which was filled with even more items. He had so many Cherokee artifacts, some of which were many years old.

During our question and answer session that day, I asked Bud what was his key to success. He thought for a moment and said, "I try to hire the best people I can find for a particular job . . . especially if they are smarter than I am."

Over the next fifteen years, I would have many occasions to interview Bud. I always found him honest with his answers . . . sometimes too honest for his own good.

### ❖ Oilers in the Hole

On July 18, 1997, the Oilers walked in the stadium known as the Hole on the campus of Tennessee State University to begin their first training camp in Nashville. Their reaction to the surroundings could be described as "shell-shocked." My first interview with Steve McNair was held sitting in a golf cart. Players such as McNair and Eddie George were given golf carts to make the trip from the Hole to the team's locker room.

Later the Oilers moved into those portable house trailers at their practice facility in Bellevue, giving it more of a shoebox than a locker room feel. It was there I first encountered the quirky personality of all-pro left tackle Brad Hopkins. "Make room . . . large naked man coming through!" he shouted, pushing his way through a gaggle of reporters.

In Hines' Sight

For the next two years, the Oilers were the NFL's version of a band of gypsies. Every game was a road game. First in Memphis, a disastrous decision, and next at Vanderbilt, which knew exactly how the Oilers felt, because the Commodores didn't have any fans either.

### ❖ And Hockey Too

Standing in Arena Plaza that day in 1997, I wondered where all these hockey fans had come from. The gathering was held to welcome NHL commissioner Gary Bettman and other league officials, who had come to Nashville to find out for themselves if our city was indeed hockey-ready and worthy of a team.

They left Music City convinced that Middle Tennessee was prepared for hockey, and in June the league granted Nashville an expansion franchise.

On October 10, 1998, the Predators took the ice for the first time at home against Florida, only to lose 1–0. It was a night, however, that signaled another giant leap for Nashville, which was rapidly experiencing a new and expanding major league culture. Three nights later, the Predators beat the Carolina Hurricanes 3–2 for their first franchise victory.

It certainly didn't happen overnight, but the Predators and major league hockey have proven over the past fourteen years how valued they are to our community by the tremendous support they have received from hockey fans and the business community. Preds players over the years have been some of the most giving and community-conscious individuals we have as a group, and that includes the front office as well.

### ❖ April 16, 1998

At 3:00 p.m., I was on the phone with my wife. I was sitting in the sports office at NewsChannel 5. Pat was home alone. The newsroom is on the lower level of the station, which is underground, so we would be insulated from the oncoming tornado our weather department said was headed straight for Channel 5. The lights began to flicker on and off. I told Pat she should run next door to the neighbors so she wouldn't be by herself. She agreed. We said we loved each other and hung up.

At about 3:30 p.m., the F3 tornado touched down near the intersection of Charlotte Pike and Forty-sixth Avenue and began ripping a path through downtown. We had photographers stationed in the lobby of our building on James Robertson Parkway shooting footage through the large plate glass windows and photographers shooting from our back door on the loading ramp.

I had gone upstairs to the second level to look outside from the loading dock just minutes before the twister passed over our back parking lot, and it was frightening. All the lights were out now, and you could hear the roaring from the high-velocity wind inside the building. As soon as it passed over Channel 5, many of us went outside and couldn't believe the utter destruction we saw.

Every available newsroom person was called into duty. I went out with a photographer to shoot footage and talk with eyewitnesses. We drove toward West End as best we could. Trees and power lines were down everywhere. It looked like a war zone. After covering West End around Vanderbilt and Centennial Park, we headed back toward town and drove over Memorial Bridge, where three huge cranes at the construction site of the Titans soon to be new home, Adelphia Coliseum, were wrecked. Total property damage to downtown Nashville would eventually be estimated at over one hundred million dollars.

Tennesseans came from all corners, and good samaritans from surrounding states rushed to our aide. The outpouring of support was tremendous, and I was proud to be part of a news organization that told the stories of so many who had lost everything in such a professional and caring way.

## ❖ Sunday Sports Central

With the addition of the Titans and Predators to the Nashville sports menu, we began a thirty-minute Sunday sports wrap-up show in 1998 called *Sunday Sports Central*. Both Channel 2 and Channel 4 also began Sunday shows about the same time, and the race was on to win the time period between the three of us. I am proud to say *Sunday Sports Central* became the dominant show on Sunday nights, due to the efforts of our entire staff, including the support of station management. A lot of energy each week went into producing that show, and the ratings reflected our dedication.

Brian McKeegan, our sports producer-photographer, led our team, which included photographer Bob Kusek and Mark Howard. Over the years, there were other folks who contributed greatly to our show, including the late Bob Rainey, Kami Carman, Eric Yutzy, Steve Layman, and Mike Rodgers.

Sometimes you knock it out of the park when you hire just the right candidate for a job. That was certainly the case when we hired Brian McKeegan. As a manager, he was my strongest ally and supporter for thirteen years, and he went out of his way to make me look good always. He now leads the NewsChannel 5 sports department with excellence. He has that intangible quality that pushes all great achievers: passion.

Photographer Bob Kusek is a wonderful example of how someone makes it happen in television. Bob came to NewsChannel 5 in 1988 as an intern. Normally interns don't want to be photographers, but Bob saw this as his ticket to a permanent job. He picked up a camera and learned to shoot, plus all the other things he does so well. Bob and I made lots of trips, and traveled many miles together. He is one of the best.

## In Hines' Sight

It was an embarrassing TV lesson learned the hard way. Bob Kusek and I were conducting interviews with Vanderbilt football players in their dressing room at Vanderbilt Stadium following a victory sometime during the 1990s. The room was crowded with players and media members. There was a lot of noise and movement. We finished our interviews and rushed back to the station to edit them for the ten o'clock news. When the sports show was over, the phones lit up. I picked up one of the calls, and before I could say NewsChannel 5 sports, the woman screamed, "How dare you put that on the air!"

Shocked, I replied, "Put what on the air, ma'am?'

"That player was naked!" she shouted.

The other calls coming into the newsroom were saying the same thing. Bob and I were dumfounded, but as soon as we looked at the video again . . . boy, were they right. In the background and over the shoulder of the player we were interviewing we saw it. In our haste to edit the interview, we hadn't noticed, but there he was, totally naked. Not what you expect to see on the ten o'clock news, huh? Guess what? We never made that mistake again.

## ❖ The Fiesta "Orange" Bowl of Champions

In January 1999, NewsChannel 5 sports producer and photographer Brian McKeegan and I flew to Tempe, Arizona, to cover the Fiesta Bowl of Champions, where Tennessee would face Florida State in the first BCS National Championship Game.

We spent a wonderful week in the desert, sending back multiple live reports with interviews from both teams each day. We even covered Phillip Fulmer and Bobby Bowden speaking at a church service on Sunday morning in Phoenix before the game on Monday.

The Vols beat Florida State 23–16 to win their first National Championship since 1951, and on the field after the game, Brian and I were engulfed in a once-in-a-lifetime college football championship atmosphere.

During the postgame press conference I experienced, for me, a first. As I interviewed Vice President Al Gore, a secret service agent firmly placed an extended arm and hand on my chest, keeping me a safe distance from the vice president. Al Gore saw what the agent was doing, and while answering a question, he kept glancing at the agent as if to say, "It's okay, I know him," but the agent never backed off. It's a good thing I didn't develop a sudden itch somewhere and attempt to scratch it, because I am certain I would have quickly been dropped to the floor.

## ❖ To Everything a Season

"There is a time for everything, and a season for every activity, under heaven" (Ecclesiastes 3:1). That season for the Titans was 1999. On August 27, the Titans walked into their new permanent home at Adelphia Coliseum to face the Atlanta Falcons in the opening preseason game. The journey home had been long and hard, and sixty thousand–plus were ready to rumble. The Titans did not disappoint, beating the Falcons and ushering in the biggest sports era in the history of Nashville.

Standing on the sidelines during the two-minute warning in the fourth quarter, I thought how special the moment was for our city and state, but little did I or anyone else anticipate the impact of the season ahead.

## ❖ The Room

Every NFL team has one. They call it *The Room*. It's the players' home away from home. An NFL locker room is a grown-up version of a romper room with sixty-one men, and there is always somebody "naked."

In most locker rooms, players watch loud TVs, listen to loud music, talk loud, and play loud games. A reporter can interview a player in various stages of dress, and sometimes you can interview a player while he is in the act of dressing, which is always a challenge. Quite often a reporter will have to wait until a player showers before an interview, then wait until he is dressed. Hopefully your deadline has not passed by then.

There are lots of reporter restrictions in the locker room. A reporter can't go looking for a player in the shower, in the weight room, in the training room, or in the players' lounge, which is a separate area from the locker room.

Members of the Titans media relations department are always hanging around listening to interviews. They want to be the first to know if a player says something he shouldn't; if he does, they might ask you not to use it. Politics, therefore, come into play. You can decide to use the soundbite, which will *not* make the media relations guys happy, meaning the next time you need a one-on-one sit-down interview with a player or coach your not playing ball will be remembered. Get the picture?

Following practice, the Titans locker room is always open to the media, but you have to be careful. Sweat-soaked jerseys fly through the air. Gobs of used ankle tape litter the floor and threaten to trip you with every step. Frustrated, disgruntled, and sometimes angry players bump into you on their way to the shower.

There is a definite locker room hierarchy, and each position has its peculiarities. Quarterbacks are sensitive people who talk when they want to—usually about once a week. Offensive lineman are always willing to talk. They need the publicity. As a group, they may be the smartest players on the team. Receivers are high-wire characters who love to talk, as long as it's about them. Tight ends are versatile athletes who usually have really big hands. They are among the best leaders on a team. NFL running backs idolize their bodies and love to show them off, and that's all I'll say about that.

Defensive linemen usually have superior and lordly attitudes to match their size. Linebackers are the crime units on defense. They are stalkers. Intellectually, they are probably the best chess players. Cornerbacks do well in Vegas. They are high-stakes gamblers with huge egos and a constant need for attention. A safety is sometimes called the quarterback of the defense. He must have the speed of a receiver combined with the aggressiveness of a linebacker. That's called a prima donna.

In summary, the locker room is the NFL's version of a very expensive Animal House . . . not unlike a few TV newsrooms I have worked in.

## ❖ Signature Moment

In forty years of covering sports, I have never witnessed anything like it. Nothing! The explosion happened on a Saturday afternoon at Adelphia Coliseum as Frank Wycheck lateraled the ball across the field to Kevin Dyson. At that moment, and for the next few seconds, the energy of sixty-seven thousand fans shook the Coliseum like an erupting volcano, and a national television audience witnessed the electrifying "Music City Miracle."

I was standing on the sidelines with Mark Howard as the play unfolded with sixteen seconds on the clock, the Titans trailing the Buffalo Bills 16–15. Dyson came charging straight toward us down the sideline 75 yards for one of the most improbable touchdowns in NFL history. It was a surreal moment for everyone in the stadium. While there was pandemonium in the stands, the officials huddled to determine if Wycheck's pass to Dyson was a lateral and not a forward pass, which would have been illegal on the kickoff. It was ruled a touchdown, and the Titans had won their first playoff game since 1991.

In the locker room after the game, Frank Wycheck was in the

middle of a sea of reporters trying to explain how "Home Run Throwback," designed by special teams coach Alan Lowery, happened.

In the next three weeks, Nashville and middle Tennessee experienced an emotional high that went beyond anything imaginable. The euphoria and excitement carried over from week to week to an unbelievable conclusion.

## ❖ The Road to Super Bowl XXXIV

I was standing in the lobby of the Titans' hotel in Indianapolis, where they would face the Colts in an AFC Divisional playoff game, when defensive line coach Jim Washburn walked up from behind and playfully pushed me. I turned to see who it was.

"You think we have a chance?" he blurted out.

"You tell me," I answered back.

"Hell, I hope so," he said. "I need to keep my job."

That was the matter-of-fact way "Wash" always talked.

"Call me after the season and let's have dinner," he said, and then he walked away.

Washburn and I had developed a unique relationship. We did end up having dinner during the summer, at one of his favorite spots, Puckett's Grocery in Leiper's Fork. Wash rode his Harley and I drove my car. Pat and I went to church with Jim and his wife, Sandy, on several Sundays, and Jim was a guest of mine on *Sportsline* several times.

Years later, during the 2005 season, I noticed Washburn seemed to be avoiding me after practice. He never looked my way or spoke. One day I approached him and asked if we had a problem.

"Hope, you can't have it both ways. You can't pretend to be my friend and trash my team on the air."

"What are you talking about?" I questioned.

"One of my players called and told me what you said."

"Okay, what did I say?"

"On your talk show several weeks ago, you said it was 'Trash the Titans' night and invited callers to have at it. You can't have it both ways." And he walked off.

The Titans were suffering through an abysmal season that year and I guess I was appealing to the bitter-emotional fan for response that night. It wasn't until training camp in August of 2006 that Washburn and I repaired our relationship.

But back to the Titans and Colts AFC Divisional playoff game. Who will ever forget Eddie George busting through the middle of the Colts' defense on his way to a second-quarter 68-yard touchdown run? Eddie rushed for a team playoff record 162 yards that day to help the Titans beat the Colts 19–16.

## ❖ A Rainy Day in Florida

One week later, on January 23, I stood in the rain at Alltel Stadium in Jacksonville and interviewed Tennessee governor Don Sundquist while owner Bud Adams and team members hoisted the AFC Championship trophy after beating the Jaguars 33–14. Jaguar fans just knew their team was going to win, and when the game was over they were the quietest, most respectful crowd of losers I ever witnessed.

## ❖ On to Atlanta

Let it be known that those seven days in Atlanta, the week of Super Bowl XXXIV, were by far the hardest I ever spent in television. We drove straight from Jacksonville to Atlanta and on Monday began eighteen-hour days for the remainder of the week. By the way, Pat had to rush to Atlanta on Tuesday to bring me clothes for the week. I didn't think to bring along enough from Jacksonville, and I certainly didn't have any warm attire.

Not only were the hours long, but it was horribly cold, and we were doing ten to fifteen live shots a day back to Nashville.

The NewsChannel 5 sports staff included me, Mark Howard, and Bob Rainey. Producer-photographer Brian McKeegan and photo journalist Bob Kusek were also there. News sent anchors Chris Clark and Vickie Yates, plus producers, reporters, photographers, and satellite truck operators. Our entire crew numbered about twenty-five, some of whom worked almost around the clock. It was great fun, but man, was it grueling.

After a week of long hours, little sleep, and freezing temperatures, on Saturday, the day before Sunday's big game, I began running a temperature and experiencing flu-like symptoms. By game time Sunday evening, my temperature was hovering around 101 degrees.

In Hines' Sight

Super Bowl XXXIV had one of the most exciting finishes in Super Bowl history. Steve McNair threw a short pass to Kevin Dyson, who was headed for the goal line to tie the game, when Rams linebacker Mike Jones tackled Dyson at the one-yard line as time expired. St. Louis won 23–16.

Sadly, I don't remember much about the game. I was in agony the entire night. My temperature had shot up to 103, and it was all I could do to stand. But, hey, this was the Super Bowl, and I had to play hurt. Was I ever hurting. Following the locker room interviews, we were set up in the parking lot outside the Georgia Dome to do a thirty-minute post-game show. I made it to the first commercial break before I handed the microphone to Mark Howard and said, "I can't go any further. You'll have to take it from here."

Someone took me back to the hotel, where I stumbled up to the room and fell in bed. My wife, who had been at the game, arrived at our room several hours later and immediately called the hotel doctor, who administered some much-needed medicine.

When Nashville held the Super Bowl parade for the Titans a few days later, I was still too sick to work and missed what would've certainly been one of the great highlights of my career. But what a season that was—the best six months I ever spent as a sportscaster.

## ❖ Music City Stars

Their names still evoke excitement from the most casual of Titan fans: Steve McNair, Eddie George, Frank Wycheck, Kevin Dyson, Derrick Mason, Jevon Kearse, Samari Rolle, Blaine Bishop, Bruce Matthews, Lorenzo Neal, and Al Del Greco.

Of all the Super Bowl XXXIV Music City Stars, perhaps Eddie George has emerged as the most fascinating following his NFL career. The Eddie of today continues to look like a Greek God, with his chiseled physique. In the past decade, he has built several businesses through George Enterprises. He is featured regularly on national radio and TV shows, and in the past few years he has become an accomplished actor. Eddie has always been very involved, as have many of his former teammates, in the Nashville community, supporting many charities and nonprofit organizations with his money and time.

Does Eddie have political ambitions? It's hard to say. He likes hanging with politicians. Pat and I were guests at the home of T. B. Boyd III and his wife, Yvette, for a Harold Ford Jr. fund-raiser, and as always Eddie was the star attraction. If he ever does decide to run for office . . . I wouldn't bet against number 27.

---

## In Hines' Sight

Nashville came alive with collective, heightened energy like never in the city's history during the Titans 1999 regular season and playoff dash to the Super Bowl. The excitement generated by a sports team arouses and stimulates a community like nothing else can. Will we ever see it again? I think so, and soon. A Stanley Cup run for the Predators is closer than ever as I write this, and the Titans are just a few key players away from another playoff season. Once a city experiences the playoff atmosphere and all the benefits that go with it . . . only repeats will satisfy.

### ❖ Joey Broke our Hearts

He died on Christmas night 2000 doing something he loved to do. Jefferson Street Joe Gilliam had a heart attack while watching the Titans and Dallas Cowboys on TV. It was the final Monday night game of the season. In four days, Joey would have been fifty. He didn't make it, but the two-time All-American quarterback from Tennessee State University had made it back from the brink of self-destruction. Drugs and alcohol had taken the former Steelers quarterback places he never intended to go. His habit was so bad in the mid '90s that he pawned his two Pittsburgh Super Bowl rings while living on the streets of Nashville. His story was a halftime feature of the Super Bowl.

Joey had a lot of friends. More than six hundred attended his funeral. I counted myself among those who loved him. I had known Joe since his days at Tennessee State. Many times he called and just wanted to talk. He would tell me where to pick him up, usually some dark, secluded area around the TSU campus. I would take him to a fast-food restaurant and order from the drive through. He never liked going inside—he was too embarrassed and was always afraid someone would see him in his current condition.

By 2000, Joe had been sober for almost three years. He had started a football camp for kids, which his dad Joe Gilliam Sr. continues today in his name. Joe was also counseling drug addicts. I had him on my TV talk show numerous times during that period, and the phone lines always lit up with callers.

I am proud to say I was given a television Emmy for the commentary I wrote and aired the week following his death. I accepted it in his name.

### A Farewell to Joe Gilliam

*Throughout the heavenly realms that day, angels whispered something extraordinary was forthcoming from God's workshop.*
*First he created an athlete's heart so full of desire.*
*Then came a body with talent only God could design.*
*God smiled, and nodded. His work was done.*
*The roar of the crowd caught his attention one day, and God looked down on the playing field at Tennessee State.*
*Just as Joey stepped into the huddle God heard him say, "Okay, boys it's first and ten. We've got 80 yards to go. Lineman, do your job, and I'll do mine cause the ball's gonna fly today."*
*The legend of Jefferson Street Joe Gilliam rose out of the Hole that day with talent so enormous all could see . . . this kid can play, and the NFL was looking his way.*
*The Pittsburgh Steelers were the lucky ones, and Joey went to Steeltown to show his stuff.*
*It wouldn't be easy, he knew. He had that label, you know. He was a quarterback, and black too.*
*The weight Joey carried on spindle legs was that of a people and a family so proud.*
*A dream was being realized, and a nation watched as Joe Gilliam blazed a trail for others who would follow.*
*Those were the days filled with highs and lows, you bet. And bad times we can't begin to imagine. Life had sacked Joey more than most.*
*It's late now in the fourth quarter, and Joey hears the cry. Get up, my son, it's not time to die.*
*With the crowds all gone and nobody watching, Joey struggled to his feet one last time as the heart of a champion began to beat.*

*He straightened up and stood tall, looked toward heaven and smiled. He had beaten the odds, and Joey had finally won.*

*So turn your heads and search the sky. And when you see that rainbow . . . you'll know.*

*There's a game in town, and Joey just threw another touchdown.*

---

## In Hines' Sight

---

We are all underdogs, every one of us, at various times and in certain situations during our lifetime. Some of us remain "dogs" for extended periods, or all of our lives, but we don't have to. That's part of the beauty of our existence. The choice is always ours. Joe Gilliam was first a "top dog" before he was ever an underdog. Which do you think he preferred?

Investigate the background of the most respected, successful person you know, or anyone of national or international prominence, living or dead. Chances are extremely favorable you will find a time in that person's life, long or short, when he or she was down.

I am constantly inspired by the final years of Joey's life, a hundred times more so than his glory years, because I personally know the struggle he waged and the battle he fought.

Jefferson Street Joe Gilliam . . . went out on top.

### ❖ Pain in Oakland

Peeing in my pants was not an option. But it almost happened at the Coliseum in Oakland during the 2002 AFC Championship game between the Titans and Raiders. I had to go really bad during half time, and there was a long line outside the press box restroom. I couldn't wait. So I charged out into the stadium looking for a sign that said MEN. After searching for several minutes, I finally spotted one. I rushed toward it like a mad man, feeling the pain with every step.

Suddenly, fear overcame me. My coat and tie didn't exactly blend in with residents of the "Black Hole," who were all around me. Card-carrying members of the Raider Nation wore silver war paint with spiked red hair. Some wore an eye patch and a black cape around their shoulders. Chains rattled all around me. I was in real trouble, because most of them were real drunk.

Some were using the urinal trough, and some were using the concrete floor. At this point it didn't really matter. Relief was the objective any way I could get it. It was at that moment that the Raider fan standing next to me pulled off his silver pirate hat and began filling it with warm "recycled beer" . . . from his bladder. When he was done, he poured the contents into the trough as best he could, placed his hat back on his head, and yelled something obscene about the Titans while raising his arms over his head . . . prominently displaying his middle finger. He then disappeared into the crowd, and I quickly slipped between two Mad Max characters at the trough just as I was about to pass out. By the way, the Titans also underwent overwhelming pain that day with their 41–24 loss to the Raiders.

❖ Frozen in New England

Some things we just don't forget. I will never, ever forget those three days in Foxborough, Massachusetts. We arrived mid-week for the 2003 AFC Divisional playoff game between the Titans and Patriots, but somebody forgot to tell us what way below freezing felt like with an in-your-face strong North wind.

Mark Howard, former Titans safety Blaine Bishop, and I had to do a thirty-minute show before the game kicked off that Saturday night, standing in the end zone at Gillette Stadium. The temperature was 4°F (–16°C). I had picked out a hat to wear, with Blaine's help. My wife absolutely hated it and will never let me forget how goofy I looked. Wearing more clothes at the same time than ever in my entire life, I looked like Frankenstein trying to walk.

Just as memorable as the temperature that night was the game's conclusion. With the Pats leading 17–14 late in the fourth quarter, the Titans had it fourth and twelve at their 47. Quarterback Steve McNair, battling the cold and his own pain, threw a pass to Drew Bennett, who went up for the ball, but couldn't bring it down. The drive died at mid-field as did the Titans' season.

## ❖ Dark Day at Daytona

It was midnight. The rain pounded the windshield as we drove out of Nashville heading to Charlotte. They would bury Dale Earnhardt the next day. Brian McKeegan and I drove all night, arriving in Charlotte early that morning to cover his funeral.

It was a huge national story. Dale Earnhardt, the best driver there ever was, the man who ruled and dominated the sport, was killed on the final turn of the final lap of the 2001 Daytona 500. Earnhardt slammed into the concrete wall just after making contact with Sterling Marlin, the 1994 and 1995 Daytona 500 winner. Hours later, Sterling was bombarded with e-mails from fans across America blaming him for Dale's death.

Marlin was devastated by the national reaction. Support came quickly, however. Sterling said, "I've had drivers call me, Nascar's called . . . and told me, 'Just hold your head up, you didn't do anything wrong.'"

Brian and I remained in Charlotte for several days, putting together stories from around Charlotte and from Earnhardt's shop in Mooresville.

On Friday, we drove to Rockingham for Sunday's Dura-Lube 400. It was there that Dale Earnhardt Jr. came to Sterling's defense during a press conference. "Sterling didn't do anything wrong," Earnhardt Jr. said, "I've looked at the tapes a hundred times, and everybody was just charging hard into the corner."

I talked with Marlin after Dale Jr.'s comments, and he was obviously relieved and thanked Earnhardt for his support. The two became good friends as a result of the tragedy and remain friends today.

## ❖ Governor's Prayer Breakfast

I got the call sometime in March 2001. Ronnie Boling was chairman of the Governor's Prayer Breakfast, and he was calling to ask if I would be the speaker at the April breakfast for Governor Don Sundquist. I was humbled and thrilled to be asked, and of course I accepted. I would be speaking to the governor, his staff, members of the legislature, and other invited guests from around the state.

Country entertainer Lee Greenwood and the Nashville Children's Choir provided the music. NewsChannel 5 Plus carried the speech live, and it will always remain one of the treasured highlights of my life.

## ❖ California Cool

Jeff Fisher would never wear Old Spice. Drive a used car. Sleep in wool pajamas. And never be caught without his sunglasses. No, Jeff Fisher is way too cool for any of that. And if his house were on fire there would be no panic. He would calmly call the fire department, explain the problem, and methodically go about gathering his most important items. Then he would probably lock the door on his way out.

In fourteen years covering Fisher I never once . . . not once, saw him agitated or rattled when talking to reporters. He always had it together. Once during a sit-down interview I tried my best to irk him by asking questions that clearly would have infuriated any other coach, but not Jeff. He just gave me that crooked half-smile and answered the questions as if he had written them.

It must have been a slow April first when, in 2003, I called Titans media director Robbie Boren and told him I wanted to do an interview with Jeff that would be an April Fool's joke. I wanted Jeff to respond to the exclusive story I was going to break that had the Titans trading both quarterback Steve McNair and running back Eddie George, plus money, to the Cincinnati Bengals for their first-round draft pick and running back Corey Dillon. The Bengals' top pick would be Heisman Trophy winner quarterback Carson Palmer.

Jeff agreed to do it, and that evening at six o'clock I aired the interview with Jeff, who was total California Cool under questioning about such an outrageous story. Our phone lines blew up immediately. What most viewers did not stick around to see, however, was at the end of the sportscast Jeff came back on, looked into the camera with a sly grin, and said, "April Fool's."

By ten o'clock that evening the story had gone national. ESPN had picked it up as did others. Some understood the story was an April Fool's joke, others didn't. I had the radio on the next morning listening to the Dan Patrick Show on ESPN, carried by 104.5 the Zone. Dan was interviewing Fisher about the April Fool's joke. The two were yukking it up, having a ball, and the Titans were getting some unusual national publicity.

## ❖ Heart + Courage = Admiration

There are great coaches, and there are great human beings. Don Meyer is both. In the weeks and months that followed a horrible car accident on September 5, 2008, everything he taught and believed tested his very being. Meyer's left leg was amputated below the knee due to his injuries. That alone might have crushed the spirit of the average person. During surgery for his injuries, however, doctors discovered he had inoperable cancer, which he continues to be treated for.

In typical Don Meyer fashion, the former David Lipscomb basketball coach returned to coach his Northern State University team for the 2008–09 season, taking the Wolves to their second straight appearance in the Division II National Tournament.

I have known Meyer since his first days at Lipscomb in 1975, and I have been as impressed with his sense of humor—which is legendary—as I was his coaching ability. I have interviewed him numerous times over the years, including on my TV talk show, and I've been a guest in his home.

Coach Meyer was presented the Jimmy V. Perseverance Award at the 2010 ESPY awards. One of the winningest coaches of any division in NCAA history, Meyer retired in 2010 after thirty-eight years of distinguished coaching.

There is no coach I hold in higher esteem than Don Meyer.

To be a team you must be a family. It is not what you teach, but what you emphasize. Prepare for every practice like you just lost your last game. Every day you teach attitude.

—Coach Don Meyer

## ❖ Learning to Be Sportscasters

Former Titan offensive tackle Brad Hopkins was the first. Then came safety Blaine Bishop, followed by quarterback Neil O'Donnell. All three received NFL distinction at their positions, and all three became NewsChannel 5 sports interns. All three wanted a career in broadcasting.

Everybody loves Brad, and I brought him on board first. Brad is Mr. Personality and was a natural on TV. He also has a passion for cars and trucks—all kinds, including classics. Every time Brad came to the station, he drove something different. You could count ten to twelve motor vehicles in his garage at any given time. On this particular day, Brad showed up in his brand new 2002 Dodge Viper. When he was leaving the station that night, he wanted me to see his new ride.

He had been bragging about the kind of take-off power the sports car had. "Watch this," he said, backing the car out of the parking lot. Except he gave it too much gas, and the car shot across the street, the rear end slamming into the concrete curve. There was a loud crunch. But Brad was having too much fun and gunned it up the street, honking the horn, as he drove out of sight.

The next time Brad came to the station, he was driving something different, and I said, "Where's the Viper?"

His face broke out in a big sheepish grin as he laughed. "You won't believe what happened," he said. "I broke the axel when I hit the curve across the street the other day. I got two blocks away and had to pull over. It wouldn't drive. I had to call a flatbed truck to come pick it up. You are the only person who knows that, and if you tell anyone I swear I'll kill you." He was joking, of course, but I don't blame him for being too embarrassed to tell anyone what happened. Now you know the rest of the story.

Blaine was a joy to work with, and as I mentioned earlier, he was part of our team at the AFC divisional playoff game between the Titans and Patriots that unforgettable frozen week in Foxborough. Over the years, Blaine has been a guest many times on different shows we have produced, and he has always been a knowledgeable addition.

Neil O'Donnell became much more than an intern. We hired Neil full time in 2007 and he became the third-string reporter for us as well as cohosting Titans Tuesday with me on NewsChannel 5 Plus for more than two years. Neil was perfect for live reports from the Titans facility during training camp each day for the six o'clock sports. He, of course, knew the game, and we had a lot of fun allowing him to demonstrate things in the field no one else could. Neil was also a pleasure to work with and a great guy to be around.

### ❖ Saturday July 4, 2009

I was sitting in my office at home on that Saturday afternoon when the phone rang. I answered. It was a close family friend. "Hope, Steve McNair is dead," she said, her voice shaking.

"What do you mean he's dead?" I responded, trying to comprehend what she had just said. I could hear people talking in the background. "Where are you?"

"I'm at a friend's pool party."

"And, how much have you had to drink?" I said sarcastically.

"I'm serious. Here, talk to my friend, who just talked to a reliable source on the scene."

After our conversation, I was totally convinced the information was true. I sat, stunned, trying to process what I had just been told. I picked up the phone and called the newsroom. Weekend producer Clay Farrer answered. "Clay have you heard that Steve McNair is dead?"

"No! Oh, my God. Is it true?"

"I'm on my way to the station. You need to try and confirm it with Don Aaron (Metro Police Public Affairs Manager) or whoever you can. Of course we need to go live with this. I'll be there in twenty minutes."

When I arrived at the station, weekend news anchor Scott Arnold was already on the air reporting what few facts were available. I joined Scott on set and we were the first station to go live with the news. For the next several hours we reported the tragic news as it became available.

Nashville was a city in shock. One of the most popular athletes ever in the state had been found dead with multiple gunshot wounds, including one to the head. Police reported that a pistol was found near the body of a woman, Sahel Kazemi, who was also shot dead inside McNair's downtown condo.

The news of McNair's death swept across the sports world like a sharp cold wind. Steve McNair's death was the ongoing top story of all the Nashville media outlets for the next week.

McNair's funeral was held the following Friday. Fans began lining up on Thursday to view McNair's closed casket at a funeral home and later at the Mount Zion Baptist Church.

Helicopters provided live TV coverage, and all of the local stations showed the memorial service live. Thousands came, including more than fifty former teammates. It was a passionate, emotion-filled service, the likes of which most of us have never witnessed.

---

## In Hines' Sight

---

I can still see that Steve McNair smile and hear that quick, funny way he laughed. I don't believe Steve ever had an enemy, not even on the opposing team. Everybody liked him, but more importantly everyone had tremendous respect for one of the toughest athletes ever, in any sport.

Steve was one of those guys you just enjoyed being around. He was always so positive and upbeat, even when he was beat up, and that was most of the time. He was a guest many times on my TV talk show. I would announce at six o'clock that he would be on later that night at eight. The phones would ring with fans asking if they could meet Steve outside for autographs. He was always one of the most popular, if not the most popular, and admired person ever on the show.

Steve was a huge bass fisherman, and he was good too. He had all the equipment, including a top of the line bass boat with all the latest technology. He and I had planned to do a fishing show sometime during the summer of 2009. He was excited about the prospect, but we never finalized a date. I count that as one of my great misfortunes.

Drop your stone the next time you write about Steve McNair. Drop your stone the next time you text somebody. Drop your stone the next time you Twitter. Drop your stone, those of you in the barbershops, the beauty shops. Those of you walking the streets on the corner, drop your stone.

What I do know about this man was that he loved God though he was just like us: imperfect.

—Bishop Joseph W. Walker III

### ❖ Raindrops Kept Falling on Our Heads

Saturday morning May 1, 2010, it rained. Sunday morning May 2, it was still raining. Then all hell broke loose, when the Cumberland River crested at 51.86 feet.

Channel 5 was a safe place to be when the tornado of 1998 hit Nashville, as the newsroom is underground. This was not so good during the 2010 flood. Like a lot of downtown businesses, our newsroom was flooded. Everybody was called in on Sunday to do what we could to save and salvage equipment, but because we were told everything the contaminated water touched had to be thrown away, there wasn't much to save. We sloshed around in boots, wearing old clothes and rubber gloves. After that, everything we wore had to be destroyed.

In the days that followed, we had to literally move our newsroom upstairs to the second level. Reporters were set up with makeshift desks in the hallways. The news producer's central office was a former meeting room, and editing equipment was set up in the back of the station next to the loading dock. The men's dressing room became the sports office, complete with our own toilet. You can guess what rule number one was: "No one uses the toilet."

The newsroom didn't miss a beat, and for more than six months we worked, like many in middle Tennessee, under trying and much less than ideal conditions. Each day we went on the air with the news of the day, and no one knew our plight.

Just as I was proud to be part of a news team that reacted with courage and professionalism during the '98 tornado, I was equally gratified to be part of an organization that reacted with the same spirit and determination during the flood of 2010. And it wasn't just us. All of middle Tennessee deserves a collective high five.

### ❖ A Few Things More

I consider myself fortunate (or peculiarly blessed) to have known two "Goats" in my lifetime. Both of them were very human, and both were extremely funny. I grew up with the first. He was Bill "Goat" Murray. We started kindergarten together and were classmates all the way through high school. The second was Billy

"Goat" Bowers, a wonderful and dear friend who constantly reminded me he was a prominent member of the original "Buckhead Boys" (Atlanta). We played many rounds of golf together. Goat Bowers claimed to have played quarterback for Georgia Tech under the legendary Bobby Dodd, and perhaps he did. I've just never found any documentation that confirms it. So, if anybody knows of a Goat Bowers who played quarterback for the Yellow Jackets, and you can prove it, please let me know.

I had to mention my dear friend Goat, because it's the only publicity he's had in fifty years. God rest his soul. I miss you, Billy, you "rambling wreck."

I have been blessed to be part of a weekly seven-man Bible study that has been meeting since 1998. Over the past fourteen years, we have become best friends. We have cried. We have laughed. Man have we laughed and cried, as we shared in each other's triumphs and downfalls. We have traveled together on golf outings and enjoyed dinners with our wives. It has been a great support group of very diverse individuals, with assorted backgrounds, who have a passionate love for Jesus Christ.

No man could belong to a better band of Boomers (Brothers Of Other Mothers). The Magnificent Seven include: Mike Arrington, Ted Bleymaier, Rob McDonald, Pete Kutz, David Miller, and Dr. Bryant Millsaps.

*Gentleman:* A cultured man who behaves with courtesy and thoughtfulness. "There will be many things in life you can't be, but the one thing I always expect you to be is . . . a gentleman." Those words were spoken by my mother many years ago. Mama would be proud to know I have been included in two groups of men whose mamas must have told them the same thing.

If you wanted to halt the wheels of commerce and cripple the power structure of Tennessee, you might consider having your army surround the beautiful estate at Hidden River Lane in Franklin, Tennessee, on the second Saturday in December. At nine o'clock in the morning, you would find several hundred highly successful movers and shakers standing around drinking mimosas and Bloody Marys. You would find them engaged in heavy posturing, offering complimentary remarks to one and all, while looking around the crowded room to see who else they needed to speak to. And there I would be, somewhere in the crowd, shaking hands, speaking highly of all I came in contact with, looking around to see who was watching me . . . the least of those with power and money. This gathering of Eagles takes place at the mansion of my good friend, prominent Tennessee banker and serial entrepreneur Gordon Inman.

For over a decade, Gordon and his wife, Shaun, have summoned his friends (some of whom are not all that rich, powerful, or famous) to what he calls a Gentlemen's Christmas Breakfast. But as Gordon says each year during his welcome speech, "All of you are here today because each of you means something special to me." One year, Gordon had all four living Tennessee governors at the breakfast, plus senators, and Auburn head football coach Tommy Tuberville.

The Gentleman's Breakfast started with Gordon and his good friend Clayton McWhorter, former president and CEO of Hospital Corporation of America. The original idea for the breakfast was to hunt quail on McWhorter's plantation in South Georgia and serve the birds as part of the breakfast meal to a gathering of friends. Each year when breakfast is over, fine cigars are offered to those who wish to remain and partake.

Gordon, by the way, is certainly no political fool. You will find both democrats and republicans at every Gentlemen's Breakfast.

The invitation reads as follows:

Gentlemen's Masters Dinner
Fine Steaks and Whiskey
Hosted by Jim Kay
5:00–8:00 p.m.
Golf Attire

Nashville attorney Jim Kay sends out this invitation to a select group of friends for Friday evening the week of the Masters golf tournament at his home in Nashville. The atmosphere is relaxed, and in this crowd of distinguished professionals, business executives, and others you are required to speak at least three languages: golf, football, and, well, the third language is optional: aches and pains or the economy.

A lot of people think they are powerful, and many act as if they wield significant authority, but I have validated proof of my power standing. I was named in the March 2000 edition of *Business Nashville* magazine's most influential people. I wasn't quite the equivalent of the NFL's last rookie chosen in the draft each year, which they call "Mister Irrelevant" . . . but I was close—number 99.

When they called and told me I would be inducted into the 2010 Nashville Fairgrounds Speedway Hall of Fame, nostalgia swept over me. I have so many great memories of times spent covering races, including the Winston Cup years with the Nascar stars of the day, plus all those hard-working local drivers and crew members who were living their dreams on Saturday nights. It was quite a show, and thanks to Tony Formosa, that same racing spirit and passion continues in 2012.

She is a woman gifted of God with the talent to teach and instill in others the discipline of winning. After all, she was only one year older than some of her players when Pat Summitt began her incredible, unbelievable journey to the very top of women's basketball as head coach at the University of Tennessee. No college coach, man or woman, has won as many games as Summitt.

Pat never stood taller than the summer of 2011, when she announced she had been diagnosed with early symptoms of Alzheimer's disease and vowed to continue coaching with this refrain: "There's not going to be any pity party, and I'll make sure of that."

It has been an honor to cover and conduct interviews over many years with Pat Summitt. She will always receive from me a loving "stare."

### ❖ Who's J.B.?

The question I have been asked most often the past twenty-five years is: "Who is J.B.?"

After reading the intro to highlights or a sound bite, during a sportscast, I would say, "Roll the tape, J.B." J.B. was Jimmy Bewley, our six and ten o'clock control room director. I used that phrase almost every sportscast, and years later when Jimmy left Channel 5, I told him that no matter who was directing the show I would continue to say, "Roll the tape, J.B." Finally, the secret is out. Even though I continued to say, "Roll the tape, J.B.," for the final fifteen years of my career at Channel 5, there was no J.B. in the house.

A number of years ago a lady wrote, chastising me for using that phrase. She stated very matter-of-factly, "How embarrassing, Mr. Hines. Doesn't J.B. know when he's supposed to roll the tape without you having to tell him every time?" I had no answer for her.

Often when people see me today, the first thing they say is, "Roll the tape, J.B.," and then they laugh. They get the biggest kick out of saying that phrase. So do I.

### ❖ Thank You

More than forty years ago, during that first 1971 summer broadcast, viewers in Middle Tennessee watched a very young, very nervous, and totally inexperienced anchor deliver his first TV sportscast. Except for an eight-year absence, middle Tennessee viewers continued to welcome me into their homes for over three decades. For that honor and privilege, I am forever indebted. We were always family, you and me. I know that because so many of you have told me so.

How blessed my family and I were to have such a tenured career at NewsChannel 5. We lived and worked in other cities, but none where the people were as accepting and giving. My heart has always been in Nashville. Because it is here the people are the finest, the air smells the sweetest, and Middle Tennessee just gets in your blood.

I am a blessed man to have such wonderful friends. I hope they know how much I value those relationships. Above all, I give

In Hines' Sight

thanks to my heavenly father who more than forty years ago made a young man's dream come true, and still does, every day in every way.

Finally, for those of you who so honored me by watching my sportscasts each night, year after year . . . the best I can possibly do is say, from my heart, THANK YOU.

## ❖ Oh, By the Way

My next book is gonna be a whole lot better than this one.

# Epilogue
## Live from New York
### April 7, 2012

*"Hope," my wife said to me on Sunday, "sit down. I want to show you something I recorded last night."*

*I said, "What is it?" Pat records a lot of HGTV shows, and I wasn't in the mood to watch someone redesign a garden or great room.*

*"It's a sketch from* Saturday Night Live, *Hope. You'll love it." Pat had watched it while I was asleep.*

*"I really don't have time to watch it now. How about later?"*

*"You're going to watch it right now," she said, and she turned it on.*

*It was a skit featuring a TV news team shooting promo shots. There were the male and female coanchors, played by Bill Hader and that evening's host, Sofia Vergara. Then there was the third member of the team, played by Fred Armisen, who was . . . wait a minute, "Hope Hines"? Me?*

*I couldn't believe what I was seeing. It was one of the funniest things I had ever seen. In the sketch, "Hope Hines" is a helicopter traffic reporter who is having trouble finding his mark for the promo shots and keeping track of where the camera is. Fred played me as a total idiot, but man, was it ever funny. Apparently, before the show that night, the writers asked the studio audience to name a sportscaster, and someone stood up and said, "Hope Hines, Channel 5 Nashville."*

*Well, all day Easter Sunday and Monday my cell phone and computer worked overtime with texts, tweets, and e-mails from people around the country. It was a hot topic on Nashville radio stations on Monday, and I spent the day making the rounds talking about the SNL sketch.*

*NewsChannel 5 even came to my home Monday afternoon and interviewed me about the sketch; the story aired during the ten o'clock news. It was one of the wildest days of my career—but wait a minute, I thought I was retired!*

## About the Author

Hope Hines enjoyed a legendary forty-year career as a television sportscaster. He won six broadcast Emmys and was named the best sportscaster in the Southeast. Hope received the Silver Circle Award from the National Academy of Television Arts and Sciences for twenty-five years of distinguished service. He and his wife, Pat, live in Nashville.

Contact Hope for speaking engagements on his website at www.hopehines.com.